Cambridge Elements

Elements in the Archaeology of Food
edited by
Katheryn C. Twiss
Stony Brook University, New York
Alexandra Livarda
Catalan Institute of Classical Archaeology

FOOD IN ANCIENT CHINA

Yitzchak Jaffe
University of Haifa

Shaftesbury Road, Cambridge CB2 8EA, United Kingdom

One Liberty Plaza, 20th Floor, New York, NY 10006, USA

477 Williamstown Road, Port Melbourne, VIC 3207, Australia

314–321, 3rd Floor, Plot 3, Splendor Forum, Jasola District Centre, New Delhi – 110025, India

103 Penang Road, #05–06/07, Visioncrest Commercial, Singapore 238467

Cambridge University Press is part of Cambridge University Press & Assessment, a department of the University of Cambridge.

We share the University's mission to contribute to society through the pursuit of education, learning and research at the highest international levels of excellence.

www.cambridge.org
Information on this title: www.cambridge.org/9781009475808

DOI: 10.1017/9781009408370

First published 2023

A catalogue record for this publication is available from the British Library

ISBN 978-1-009-47580-8 Hardback
ISBN 978-1-009-40838-7 Paperback
ISSN 2754-2971 (online)
ISSN 2754-2963 (print)

Food in Ancient China

Elements in the Archaeology of Food

DOI: 10.1017/9781009408370
First published online: December 2023

Yitzchak Jaffe
University of Haifa

Author for correspondence: Yitzchak Jaffe, yjaffe@univ.haifa.ac.il

Abstract: This Element provides an overview of food and foodways in Ancient China, from *Homo sapiens* (around 50 KYA) up to its historical beginnings: the foundation of the Zhou dynasty (at the start of the first millennium BCE). While textual data provide insights on food and diet during China's historical periods, archaeological data are the main source for studying the deep past and reconstructing what people ate, how they ate and with whom. This Element introduces the plants and animals that formed the building blocks of ancient diets and cuisines, as well as how they created localized lifeways and unifying constructs across Ancient China. Foodways – how food is grown, prepared and consumed – were central in the development of differing social, economic and political realities, as they shaped ritual and burial practices, differentiated ethnic groups, solidified community ties and deepened or assuaged social inequalities.

Keywords: food, China, ancient, archaeology, Chinese

ISBNs: 9781009475808 (HB), 9781009408387 (PB), 9781009408370 (OC)
ISSNs: 2754-2971 (online), 2754-2963 (print)

Contents

Preface

In the University of Haifa library system, you will find the food section sandwiched between the ones on marriage and death. Readers can come up with their own witticisms here, but a classification system where food is the main course between coupling and our eventual demise is not all that irrational. As I write these sentences, my father-in-law is calling his wife, for what must be the fifth time now, to come downstairs and have lunch with him. Even as the food is getting cold, he will not eat it alone, nor would he want my mother-in-law to. (Although I suspect she would not mind it all that much; she has work to do and needs to get back to it.) From the daily meal to the wedding feast, food is a fundamental part of our lives and a central aspect of our social existence; far more than a source of fuel for the physical body, food – how we cook it, eat it and perhaps most importantly with whom we share it – is wrapped up in the many political, economic and social aspects of our lives.

That food is central to Chinese culture and civilization is a worn-out trope that will be repeated here only this once. Obtaining daily nourishment is the foundation for the development of cooking and preserving techniques upon which distinct flavors and regional kitchens evolved. High cuisine has long been an important indicator to differentiate important lords from members of the lower classes and diets as a crucial marker distinguishing "us and them." Food was a common figurative device to convey political lessons and philosophical metaphors (for an overview on these topics, see Sterckx 2004).

This Element is about food in Ancient China. Textual evidence, artistic representations and the rare preserved meal aid in reconstructing food and society for the better-known historical periods. Our main data source here will be archaeology, as it is the only one we have for the deep past and because it provides a fantastic set of tools and methods, for any time period, with which to reconstruct what people ate, how they ate and with whom. Readers with little prior knowledge in the field can find good overviews on Chinese history and archaeology in English in Liu and Chen (2012), Underhill (2013), Shelach (2015) and Goldin (2018). Whenever possible I have tried to include entries from the growing body of scientific work published in English-language journals, and those seeking original site reports and further elaboration in Chinese can consult their bibliographies as well as the aforementioned volumes.

1 Introduction

Ancient China: What, When and Where

What, when and where is Ancient China? Starting with this set of questions might seem odd, but the way we answer them directly shapes how we study food in Ancient China. First off, the question of what is Ancient China is connected to the question of when is Ancient China, as in when did China emerge as the social and cultural entity we are more familiar with today? This question has a number of answers to be sure, and each depends on how we define China and its constitutive elements (language, artistic styles, food etc.) that subsequently enable us to assess where and when this or that element emerged. From a food and cuisine perspective we can think of certain hallmarks of Chinese cuisine and ask when they first appeared or were conceived. For example, when were chopsticks first used? But we quickly run into a second set of questions. How central, really, are chopsticks to our definition of China (does it stop being Chinese food when consumed with a fork)? Are chopsticks enough? In other words, if falafel balls are eaten with chopsticks, do they no longer count as Middle Eastern food?

The what and the when of Ancient China are further connected to the question of where Ancient China is. Simply using modern borders is not without issue either, as cultural zones and official political borders have shifted over time. Chinese polities have contracted and expanded considerably in the past, resulting in stark changes in the landmass they inhabited, influenced and controlled at different periods. Traditional narratives view Ancient China as developing in the Yellow River Valley and spreading out to engulf the surrounding regions that make up its modern-day boundaries (see Map 1). These models were later supplanted by ones espousing multiple endemic and independent lines of development, each in a different geographic area. Only later, around the late second or first millennium BCE (aka the Bronze Age), had they converged to form a single all-important center from which Chinese civilization eventually emerged. This is an especially important period in the development of Chinese civilization – historical texts describe the pre-imperial time as one of a succession of dynasties – the Xia, Shang and Zhou – their dates roughly corresponding to the first and second millennia BCE. Consequently, the term "Ancient China" has different meanings: the period of time prior to the afore-mentioned three dynasties (i.e., pre second millennium BCE), or as beginning in the second millennium BCE and extending into the first as in up until the end of the Zhou period and the start of the imperial era (at 221 BCE with the Qin unification). Often, the late Shang, but mainly the Zhou period, or the first millennium BCE, marks the starting point of Chinese civilization as it is when many hallmarks of later Chinese culture, art and style and, importantly, a developed written language, can be identified for the first time (see discussions in Goldin 2018, Liu & Chen 2012, Shelach 2015 and Underhill 2013).

A recent survey of publication trends in Chinese archaeology shows that these periods, and the cultures and sites they reflect, are still the most intensively

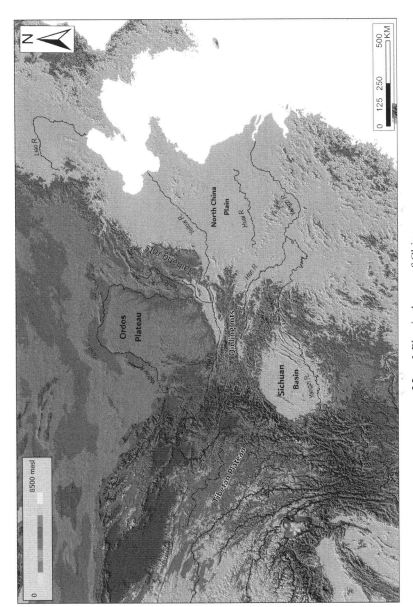

Map 1 Physical map of China

researched and published (Wei et al. 2022). Accordingly, the geographic areas where the three dynasties are thought to have emerged and later developed receive more attention as well, notably the Yellow and Yangzi River valley plains – China's two great river systems – in the provinces of (in alphabetical order) Henan, Hubei, Jiangsu, Shaanxi, Shandong and Shanxi. The geography of China is also at the center of the many regional and macro cuisines that make China the modern tapestry of foods and flavors it is today. They are as much the products of cultural traditions and the desire or ability to engage with foreign influences, as they are those of environmental conditions available to the people inhabiting its diverse ecological zones.

China is a vast country (a subcontinent, really, and the fourth largest country in terms of landmass) comprised of a diverse array of ecological, environmental and topographic zones crisscrossed by numerous rivers and multiple mountain ranges (Map 1). In general, as one moves north, the climate gets colder and drier and the variation between the seasons greater. It is common to divide North and South China along a line that runs from east to west along the Qinling Mountains and separates the Yellow and Yangzi Rivers as well as their fertile valleys. The north is, on average, colder and drier than the hotter and more humid south, which receives annual rainfall averages of more than 1,000 mm (some places nearing 2,000 mm) and remains above freezing year-round. China can be further divided along an east–west axis where the flatter fertile loess lands, suitable for agricultural production, can be found in the east, a region where the climate is further mediated by the vicinity to the Pacific Ocean. In the west, the Tibetan Plateau abuts the fertile Sichuan Basin – China's other breadbasket. Beyond, in Gansu, Ningxia and Xinjiang to the northwest, barren deserts extend for hundreds of kilometers. In an even longer band that runs across China's northern edge, the steppe plains form a sea of grass so cold and dry it makes agriculture equally nearly impossible; here is where, later on, pastoral and seminomadic lifeways emerged.

Knowing which plants and animals existed in the past and would have been available for consumption is crucial. Yet here again we know that conditions in the past differed from those we observe today. The line defining the north–south divide shifted considerably over time and was influenced by the varying strength of the annual winter and summer monsoon rains, which in turn influenced which species of plants and animals could survive and thrive. Other changes were human-made. As China's population grew, forests were cleared and turned into agricultural lands at the expense of indigenous wildlife. Mark Elvin (2004) famously suggested that elephants, so abundant throughout what is now much of modern-day China, were gradually pushed south until, in the late nineteenth century, they almost became extinct (for an updated ecological history of China, see Lander 2021).

These changes are to be expected. Geographic conditions and climates have shifted. I ask readers to keep in mind that the economy, culture, social and political systems have changed as well. Fittingly, then, this is not an Element about ancient Chinese food, but one on food during ancient times in the area we now call China. We will be focusing on periods of human occupation in the Paleolithic era and end on the eve of historical China at the late second millennium BCE. Excellent works have focused on reconstructing the food of China during the later historical eras (e.g., Anderson 1988; Höllmann 2014; Sterckx 2004). Often, they turn to the available historical and imperial periods using the ample surviving texts, images and art historical data as guides for their studies (see Section 2). The lack of any contemporaneous texts for periods earlier than those of Shang Anyang (~1250–1050 BCE, where the famous oracle bones provide a wealth of inscriptional evidence) makes the reconstruction of the silent, deep past quite challenging. The salience afforded to narratives and basic information found in later historical texts, even those elaborating on prehistory, especially prior to the first millennium, is contentious and doubly so once we go further back in time to periods removed several millennia from any written record. Thankfully, archaeology provides a powerful lens to evaluate food in prehistoric periods. It has been steadily supplying unparalleled information on the foodstuffs comprising diets, how cuisine has evolved and how endemic cultivation practices, together with external influences, have continued to shape culinary developments.

Reconstructing Foodways in Ancient China: An Archaeological Approach

The stone rubbing pictured in Figure 1 depicts a busy Han dynasty kitchen. We see cooks skirting around large bubbling cauldrons, some placed on a stovetop, others on an open fire. A variety of animals are being prepared, large fowl hang from a rack and a cow's head is clearly visible. Cooks and assistants are busy mixing ingredients, adding liquids and stirring pots.

Recipes and dishes, their general ingredients and preparation methods, also survive. Some of the first are as early as the first half of the first millennium BCE. The *geng* meat soup enjoyed by commoners and nobles alike is at the center of moral discourses on matters of the state in this Zuozhuan passage (translation in Chang 1977, 51):

> Harmony may be illustrated by soup. You have the water and fire, vinegar, pickle, salt, and plums, with which to cook fish and meat. It is made to boil by the firewood, and then the cook mixes the ingredients, harmoniously equalizing the several flavors, so as to supply whatever is deficient and carry off whatever is in excess.

Figure 1 Kitchen scene from Dahuting tomb, Henan. Eastern Han dynasty
(25–220 BCE) (Wang & Yu 1972, 61)

The lively picture provides invaluable insight into Han dynasty high-elite
kitchen life, and political philosophy treatises conjure up dishes so vividly
one's mouth begins to water. These are some of the earliest imagery and textual
evidence we have for food in China, and while it is tempting to use this as
a guide for earlier periods in this Element, we will not turn to them for several
reasons. First, a number of excellent sources in English on this topic can already
be consulted. K. C. Chang's (1977) edited volume is still a first-rate account of
food in Ancient China from a traditional perspective. When dealing with earlier
periods, especially the Neolithic era (and rarely earlier), however, there is much
less to say, and studies often rely heavily on later historical information to
reconstruct the less-known deeper past. This is perfectly acceptable if we are
interested in understanding when stir-fry was first practiced or if we are trying to
pin down the earliest evidence we have for the centrality of oyster sauce in
Chinese cuisine. Yet this can often be counterproductive as it espouses continu-
ity and little change in China's past and potentially overlooks the many ways
different foods were enjoyed. In fact, the period of time prior to the Zhou has
seen far more studies pertaining to food, cuisine and diet – a result of explicit
research foci, themselves shaped by the existence of larger amounts of textual
evidence during this period (with most dated to the later centuries).

Unexpected and even unimaginable realities are uncovered once we unburden
ourselves of the need to fit early data into models and narratives of later pasts. Only
recently have scholars shown that during the Paleolithic era, and for thousands of
years before agriculture was on anyone's mind, acorns, the fruit of the oak tree,
were an important meal item being gathered, consumed and even stored in bulk

(Section 2). Some later historical texts and narratives have also clouded the way we reconstruct cuisines in the past. To the north of China's traditionally viewed "central zones" is an area often described in historical texts as inhabited by nomadic pastoralists, whose diets centered around ruminant meat and fat and very little grain. This might have been the staple cuisine of the Xiongnu, China's off-and-on-again enemies throughout the later Han dynasty, but recent work has shown that the diet of the people who inhabited this region before them was more varied and complex than this simple characterization (Section 5).

The plants and animals available to the ancients formed the building blocks of their cuisines. Thankfully, this is something archaeologists can identify more readily in the material record – bones and seeds can often be found in archaeological sites and provide direct evidence for the grains grown and the animals they hunted or raised. As we will see, millet and rice were indeed grown in different ecological zones, but some communities during the Neolithic era chose or had to grow both (Section 3), while others welcomed the introduction of barley and wheat, which enabled them to inhabit less forgiving climates (Section 5).

Ingredients on their own can take us only so far. Anyone flying commercial knows that chicken or beef is as much a question of availability as it is a matter of taste and preference. It is true that a society subsisting on wheat as opposed to one centered around rice will further require different farming strategies for planting, harvesting and storing, as well as processing and consuming the grain – all of which will in turn influence and shape the seasonal and annual rhythms of community life, as well as structure familial and social relationships and even political and economic systems. But we would undoubtedly deride future archaeologists if they were to lump all European cuisines together when they discovered that most were centered around wheat consumption. Wheat is used to bake bread, cakes and pies, boil pasta and whole grain gruel in an endless array of tastes and traditions that are at the heart of local, regional or national identities. Still, pasta is often made of durum wheat, unlike the hardy winter wheat used to make traditional German bread, providing the clues that archaeologists often have access to, but they can be used in more ways than one. The way grain is milled into flour or rough semolina to make pasta or finely ground to bake bread is the main difference between the cuisines and dishes in our example. In fact, semolina is used to make pasta, cakes, porridge, dumplings, couscous or, my favorite, kibbeh (the Kurdish kind, boiled in a sweet-and-sour soup, thank you!) – a small selection that begins to get at the myriad ways in which the same grain can be used to distinguish innumerable cuisines (and, of course, one can always just boil the berries and add them to a salad – I hope this point is clear).

Moving from ingredients to cuisine is challenging, but whenever possible I present studies that engage with foodways. There are a number of ways to define the term *foodways*. For our purposes here, I employ Reed's (2021) broad definition of food systems, one that encapsulates all the activities and aspects involved in feeding a society, including, but not limited to, growing, harvesting, storing, processing, transporting, cooking, consuming and discarding food. All of these components are related to and entangled in social, political, economic and ritual aspects (to name a few), which involve, in turn, a range of actors and institutions at differing levels and scales. Additionally, what is added to each dish, how it is prepared and spiced, when it is served and who gets to eat it, as well as how often, join to create different foodways.

Can archaeology provide information on these (or at least some) of these aspects? Absolutely (see Hastorf 2016, Twiss 2019)! The tried and true staples of environmental archaeology, zooarchaeology and archaeobotany (the study of ancient plant and animal remains) together with paleoclimatology (the study of past climates) help us reconstruct past environments and the flora and fauna available to ancient societies. Reconstructing ancient landscapes and environments is an ongoing endeavor and insights into changing climatic conditions can be gauged by tracking the habitation extent of wildlife, for example. When *Hystrix*, a genus of porcupines adapted to warmer climates, are identified, they can be taken to preclude arctic conditions in the past (Tong 2008). Careful excavation and documentation of wildlife remains aids in the reconstruction of the types of plants and animals humans exploited, as well as their relative dietary proportion. The introduction of new techniques, geometric morphometrics, characterization of peptide sequences of protein biomarkers (aka ZooMS), ancient DNA studies and microscopic starch and phytolith analysis provide archaeologists with evidence for food ingredients even when macroscopic remains are limited. The combination of organic residue analysis and use-alteration inspection of flint tools, ceramic vessels, stone grinding implements and agricultural equipment reveal how food was grown, harvested and processed, and even cooked and served. For example, millet, which is today mostly consumed as cooked porridge or steamed into buns, can also be ground into flour and shaped into noodles, possibly enjoyed as early as the Middle Neolithic era (Section 5).

Archaeology can also provide excellent understandings on how food growing, eating and discarding shaped social and political systems as well as the identities of the people who practiced them. Cooking and eating are inextricably involved in gender norms, shaping and maintaining group identities, rank and just plain old taste. The tools used to hunt, gather and process food were quite diverse during the Paleolithic era. Some developments suggest technological progress and processing efficiency; others reflect local knapping traditions.

Frequently, diets varied in accordance to local tastes and preferences (Section 2). Alcohol and meat were often widely shared, but sometimes restricted, fostering community solidarity as well as deepening social divides (Section 4). Food moved great distances across the ancient landscapes, finding its way to the tables of commoners and elites alike (Section 5).

In this Element, we will mostly be moving forward in time, from Paleolithic beginnings up until the very start of China's historical periods: the Zhou of the first millennium BCE. Each section is further divided into subsections providing an outline of important developments, such as plant domestication or the invention of pottery, and overviews of foodway systems, such as urban provisioning and the social utility of feasts. This will not be an exhaustive account by any means. My aim is not only to present the diets and cuisines of the past, but to argue that food is a powerful way to study the development of ancient societies as well. Focusing on how foodways changed and how they in turn continually shaped people and communities in the past is to review many of the central aspects of economic and political growth and the major milestones in the development of human societies that made up China's ancient landscape.

A final word on dates, names and locations: the names of important sites (and some cultures) are accented in bold and their location is described via modern-day provincial settings (e.g., **Anyang** is found in modern-day Henan) – anything beyond that would burden you the reader as it would require several maps drawn to different scales (Map 2 and Table 1).

I provide names in the Pinyin transliteration from Chinese into Latin letters. Dates are presented in the form of BCE (Before the Common Era) only for most sites and periods even when calibrated BP or dates exist, since many do not have such information. In the first subsection of Section 2, "Paleolithic Beginnings," dates are also given in KYA (thousands of years ago). I believe together they will help readers keep track of both time and place while avoiding encumbering readers with too many details.

No single Element can comprehensively cover the entirety of twenty-first-century archaeology in China. The sites and remains addressed in this Element have been selected due to their representation of some of the most significant and well-known findings from their respective periods and regions. Many of these sites have undergone extensive study and have been efficiently documented, making them suitable for in-depth investigations related to food presented in this Element. Certain sites were chosen as they offer the earliest examples of specific food-related or culinary practices, or serve as exemplars showcasing the diversity within what may initially appear to be a homogeneous landscape of dietary or culinary traditions. The data presented in this Element, although not exhaustive, collectively provide a comprehensive overview of the

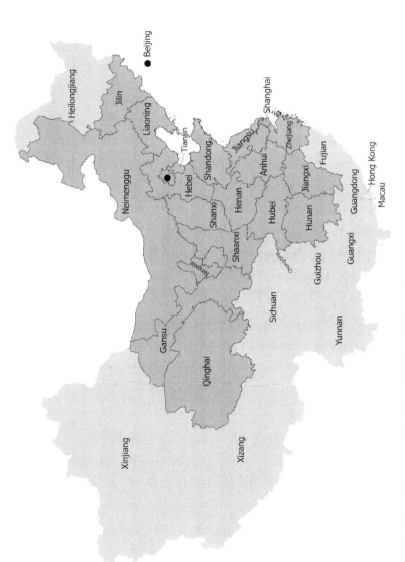

Map 2 Administrative map of mainland China. Main provinces overviewed in the text are highlighted in color.

Table 1 Sites mentioned in the text

Site name	Chinese name	Province/area	Section
Lingjing	灵井	Henan	2
Fuyan	福岩洞	Hunan	2
Nihewan cluster	泥河湾遗址群	Hebei	2
Tianyuan	田园洞	Beijing	2
Jinsitai	金斯泰	Inner Mongolia	2
Zhoukoudian	周口店	Beijing	2
Shuidonggou cluster	水洞沟遗址群	Ningxia	2
Shizitan	柿子滩	Shanxi	2
Longwangchan	龙王辿	Shaanxi	2
Xianrendong	仙人洞	Jiangxi	2
Yuchanyan	玉蟾岩	Hunan	2
Houtaomuga	后套木嘎	Jilin	2
Donghulin	东胡林	Beijing	2
Nanzhuangtou	南庄头	Hebei	2
Hutouliang	虎头梁	Hebei	2
Lijiagou	李家沟	Henan	2
Shangshan	上山	Zhejiang	2
Bianbiandong	扁扁洞	Shandong	2
Jiahu	贾湖	Henan	3
Pengtoushan	彭头山	Hunan	3
Bashidang	八十垱	Hunan	3
Tianluoshan	田螺山	Zhejiang	3
Kuahuqiao	跨湖桥	Zhejiang	3
Chahai	查海	Liaoning	3
Xinglongwa	兴隆洼	Inner Mongolia	3
Zhaobaogou	赵宝沟	Inner Mongolia	3
Houli	后李	Shandong	3
Yuezhuang	月庄	Shandong	3
Xihe	西河	Shandong	3
Zhangmatun	张马屯	Shandong	3
Xiaojingshan	小荆山	Shandong	3
Hemudu	河姆渡	Zhejiang	4
Niuheliang	牛河梁	Liaoning	4
Dadiwan	大地湾	Gansu	4
Xipo	西坡	Henan	4
Yuchisi	尉迟寺	Anhui	5
Dawenkou	大汶口	Shandong	5
Shimao	石峁	Shaanxi	5

Table 1 (cont.)

Site name	Chinese name	Province/area	Section
Taosi	陶寺	Shanxi	5
Zhoujiazhuang	周家庄	Shanxi	5
Zhaimaoliang	寨峁梁	Shaanxi	5
Liangchengzhen	两城镇	Shandong	5
Liangzhu	良渚	Zhejiang	5
Xinzhai	新砦	Henan	5
Dongzhao	东赵	Henan	5
Lajia	喇家	Qinghai	5
Miaoliang	庙梁	Shaanxi	5
Sanzuodian	三座店	Inner Mongolia	5
Huizuiwa	灰嘴瓦	Gansu	5
Zhanqi	占旗	Gansu	5
Erlitou	二里头	Henan	6
Zhengzhou	郑州	Henan	6
Yanshi	偃师	Henan	6
Anyang	安阳	Henan	6
Guandimiao	关帝庙	Henan	6

state of the field regarding foodways in ancient China at the time of writing. Figure 2 provides the basic ceramic types archaeologists in China have used to describe material culture agglomerations. Readers can refer to it as a general guide – when possible I include specific illustrations or pictures.

Regarding the terms "Ancient China" and "Chinese," it is helpful to think of the periods before the Zhou period (~1050–221 BCE) – that is, those covered in this Element – along the lines of how Yuri Pines has viewed them: "the term 'Chinese' . . . may be justifiably criticized as both anachronistic and misleading. 'Chinese' of course is a Western term" (Pines 2005, 63). Like Pines, I use the term "Chinese" here as a conventional norm and as a handy term for ease of presentation that refers to ancient foodways in the area we now know as China.

2 The Deep Past: From Gatherer-Hunters to the First Farmers

Paleolithic Beginnings

How modern humans, *Homo sapiens*, arrived and developed in China is hotly debated. Opinions vary on whether early populations replaced existing hominins or developed locally from existing groups of *H. erectus*. The earliest modern human populations are found in South and Central China, but their dates are not

Figure 2 Common generic ceramic vessel forms (not to scale, created by Rong Fan). 1. Yan 甗; 2. Ding 鼎; 3. Dou 豆; 4. Li 鬲; 5. Gaobingbei 高柄杯; 6. Fu 釜; 7. Guan 罐; 8. Bo 钵; 9. Sanzubo 三足钵; 10. Shuangerguan 双耳罐; 11. Bei 杯; 12. Hu 壶; 13. Zun 尊; 14. Qigai 器盖; 15. Pen 盆; 16. Beihu 背壶; 17. He 盉; 18. Gui 鬶

settled either. Some evidence points to 130–120 KYA (and see recent overview in Dennell et al. 2020), but ancient DNA studies suggest that all modern human populations share genetic ancestry with an African group that populated the world after 60 KYA, thus questioning these early dates (Sun et al. 2021).

Here, we will limit ourselves to asking what the earliest humans hunted, gathered and subsisted on. Early human populations would have relied on locally available animals and plants, though usually only the remains of the former, bones, survive in the material record. Stone tools, provide invaluable information on hunting and gathering and although plants do not survive as well (nor do wooden tools or leather equipment), and new techniques can identify their remains and even provide insight into how these ingredients were processed and consumed. Early sites are dominated by large mammal remains. At **Lingjing** in Henan (~125 KYA), rich remains of gazelle (*Procapra*), deer (*Cervus* and *Megaloceros*), wild ass (*Equus hemionus*), wild horse (*Equus caballus*), wild cattle (*Bos*) and rhinoceros (*Coelodonta*) were found (Li et al. 2017). The cave site of **Fuyan** (aka Daoxian ~120–80 KYA) in Hunan yielded remains from thirty-eight animal species, some now extinct, including the giant panda (*Ailuropoda melanoleuca baconi* though unclear if they were consumed by humans), large bovids (*Bos gaurus*) and saber tooth tigers (*Panthera tigris*), alongside boar (*Sus scrofa*), tapirs (*Tapirus augustus*) and smaller mammals such as otters (*Lutra lutra*), porcupines (*Hystrix*) and the bamboo rat (*Rhizomys*; Li et al. 2019b; Liu et al. 2015). Plant remains have not been found, but several of the preserved human teeth had cavities. If indeed South China was a point of entry for early human populations, the new diet they shifted to in the semi-tropical forests might have resulted in the development of tooth decay (Dennell et al. 2020). A recent study looking at dental calculus remains suggests these human populations consumed a variety of nuts, tubers, roots and grass seeds, chief among them acorns (Wu et al. 2022a).

In northern China, the **Nihewan** site cluster shows intermittent occupation by a range of hominin groups throughout the Pleistocene. Horses, onagers and gazelles were extensively hunted by members of the *Homo* genus for hundreds of thousands of years. During cold periods wooly rhinoceros, horses and mammoth (*Mammuthus trogontherii*) roamed the landscape, while warmer periods allowed archaic forms of bovines (*Leptobos stenometopon*) and deer to thrive (Yang et al. 2020). Robust skeletal evidence for early *H. sapiens* is found at sites near Beijing, such as **Tianyuan** cave ~40 KYA where various deer are dominant (Shang et al. 2007). Stable isotope analysis on skeletal remains point to a diet heavy in meat and possibly fish (Hu et al. 2009). Other groups targeted specific animal taxa. At the **Jinsitai** site (~47–37 KYA) in Inner Mongolia for example, wild horse constitute more than 60 percent of the bone assemblage (Li et al. 2018a).

Microblades and the Question of Behavioral Modernity

For decades, the transition from the Middle to Upper Pleistocene (~50 KYA) in Western Asia and Europe was coupled with a marked change in material culture, believed to have emerged when *H. sapiens* achieved their ascendency over Neanderthals. The main signifiers included technological developments of lithic assemblages, especially the production of blades and later bladelets, but also the new ability to work bone and antler, and the creation of symbolic art, such as cave paintings, ornate beads and pendants. Collectively, these practices were seen as typifying modern behavior, further reflecting developed cognitive faculties that indicated a qualitative shift in mental capacity and a new cultural development of the Upper Paleolithic (Bar-Yosef 2002). Other scholars pointed out that many of these hallmarks were actually older than 50 KYA and found in Africa as well, and thus cannot be taken to indicate a large change (including genetic) that took place during this time (see Mcbrearty and Brooks 2000).

China did not, initially, play much of a role in this debate (which has, it should be noted, evolved and changed quite a bit since its inception). For one, it had not seen the same level of prehistoric exploration other parts of the world enjoyed and many gaps existed in its Paleolithic record. The situation has changed dramatically in recent years. Excavations have uncovered Acheulian handaxes and Mousterian blades, until then thought absent (Li et al. 2018a; Qu et al. 2013). Evidence for early bone tool production can be found as early as 35 KYA in Guizhou Province, southern China (Zhang et al. 2016) and at the upper cave locales of contemporaneous **Zhoukoudian** in the north, personal ornaments have been found including perforated animal teeth of badgers (*Meles* sp.), foxes (*Vulpes vulgaris*, *V. corsac*), several types of deer and even tigers. Ornaments were made of fish bone and mollusks, further indicating the variation, possibly, of food sources (d'Errico et al. 2021).

Microliths, small bladelets shaped by retouch and inserted into hafts for various uses, hold a special place in discussions on diet and subsistence practices and were a key aspect of the behavioral modernity debate. Stone tools are first and foremost a means to procure and process food resources. Changes in tool assemblages, and the transition to small microlithic industries, can therefore be seen as reflecting changes in subsistence patterns, not just stylistic developments of knapping traditions (for Nihewan, for example, see Yang et al. 2020). Some scholars argue that unlike larger flaked tools, microliths, often no more than a few centimeters in size, can more easily be used as projectile points or tools for boring holes. They also allow for new ways of hafting. If they are used to make arrows, fitted into a good bow, new animals can be hunted from a safe distance. Pressure on lithic resources, access to quality flint or competition over limited resources, could lead to the knapping of smaller tools, but there are also other considerations that would lead societies to produce them: some have suggested that microblade cores are relatively small and can be carried around to quickly produce a tool for a specific task, and thus might be favored by hunter-gatherers exploiting variable resources. Others advocate that microliths provide a strategy for risk reduction, since multifunctional tools can aid in acquisition of foodstuffs in an uncertain environment. The flexibility and versatility of microliths allow groups to acquire a wider selection of food resources in contrast to specialized tool production, where groups focus on a select number of animals or plant species. Microliths might further encourage the production and use of labor-intensive hafting tools as they can be swapped in and out of handles when a cutting edge is worn out (see overview in Elston & Brantingham 2002). Whatever their advantages, microliths need to be evaluated on a case-by-case basis.

Microblade technologies are found across a number of sites in China, possibly as early as ~40 KYA, at the **Shuidonggou** cluster in Ningxia (Peng et al. 2014).

Sites here were occupied intermittently over tens of thousands of years and changed over time. During the earlier periods, human groups targeted larger "high-yield" animals, such as gazelle (*Procapra przewalskii*), deer, horse and water buffalo (*Bubalus* sp.), but over time they included "lower-yielding" small game: hares (*Lepus* sp.), birds and rodents, suggesting a broader spectrum of hunted species (Yi et al. 2021b). Other early evidence for microliths comes from the site of **Shizitan** S29 in Shanxi (~29–25 KYA) (Song et al. 2019b), character-ized by long periods of occupation, with tens of thousands of stone tool artifacts, thousands of animal bones and nearly 300 hearths. Various animal species were exploited at different periods, with varying numbers of gazelle, horse, bovines and deer (Song et al. 2017). Changing environmental conditions may have shaped these trends as some animals, such as horse and the now extinct *Bos primigenius*, preferred open grasslands, while other species of deer prefer warmer forested settings. Microlithic specialization may have aided in successfully hunting these animals. At **Longwangchan** (~29–25 KYA) in Shaanxi, microlithic technology is well evidenced and could indicate a shift from favoring large mammals to a more opportunistic hunting regime targeting smaller animals and wider varieties of plants and nuts, possibly during a period when the climate was cold and dry (Zhang et al. 2011). Further evidence for this broad-spectrum subsistence style, and possibly the need to process more types of food, is the finding of one of the earliest examples of grinding slabs in China, where the remains of the Paniceae family, possibly wild millets, were identified (Yang et al. 2018b).

Microliths are a North China phenomenon and would become more preva-lent toward the end of the Pleistocene. Many sites in the north are dominated by hare and gazelle that may not have required a new technological innovation to hunt. In South China, which remained warmer throughout most of the later part of the Pleistocene and into the Holocene, favorable climatic conditions would have put less stress on existing flora and fauna to require a development or adaptation of specialized clothes. Another possible explanation for why microliths may not have been needed to satisfy dietary needs in the south is that local resources, mainly bamboo (which does not survive well archaeo-logically), could have been easily fashioned into a number of tools with the simple cobble and flake industries (Bar-Yosef et al. 2012) – but this remains unverifiable.

Developments in Food-Processing Technologies: Ceramics and Grinding Stones

Absence of microblades had little to do with a lack of creativity, for the earliest ceramic vessels in the world come from South China, at the cave sites of

Xianrendong (~20 KYA Wu et al. 2012) and **Yuchanyan** (~18 KYA Boaretto et al. 2009). These early ceramics are U or V shaped, low fired, thick walled and heavily tempered with plant fiber, sand, shell or quartz, all characteristics making them better suited for cooking over direct fire sources. A small number of rice remains have been found at Xianrendong, and the animal assemblage was dominated by various types of deer, boar and rodents (Cohen et al. 2017). Fauna at Yuchanyan is similar, with the addition of aquatic birds (Prendergast et al. 2009). In the north, ceramics appear much later, around 11–10 KYA. It is unclear if these ceramics were conceived independently or connected to a separate early ceramic tradition found along the Russian far eastern coast (Wang & Sebillaud 2019).

Knowing why and when the first ceramics were made is one thing, but understanding what they were used for is quite another. Early models hypothesized a close connection between the transition to agriculture and the formation of sedentary lifestyles. Because grains, believed to have been the main domesticates cultivated by the earliest farmers, cannot be eaten raw, societies needed an implement to reliably cook the grains that came to be so reliant on them. What we now know about sedentism, agriculture and ceramics seriously undermines this theory (see Shelach-Lavi & Tu 2017). Pottery does seem to appear quite some time after domestication occurs in the Levant; however, ceramics predated established sedentary agricultural communities in other regions of the world, most notably China (Jordan & Zvelebil 2009). Second, it is now clear that agriculture developed over a long time; thousands of years would pass from the initial cultivation of plants and animals until their full domestication and the final full-scale adoption of agriculture as the primary source of sustenance for human populations across the globe (see Section 3).

Some have pointed out that since gatherer-hunter groups increasingly consumed wild acorns (*Quercus* sp.) and grains well before their initial cultivation, the earliest ceramic vessels may still have been used to detoxify and prepare plants for consumption (see chapter 2 in Shelach 2015). Grinding stones and other pounding stone tools predate the domestication and cultivation of plants as well, though they too were used to process wild specimens. At the Shizitan site cluster in Shanxi Province, harvesting of wild cereals (such as acorns, wild grasses and other tubers and root plants Liu et al. 2011) was practiced by mobile hunter-gatherer groups without sedentary dwellings, who were extensively exploiting (grinding and possibly baking) wild resources thousands of years before they were domesticated.

Grinding stones would have allowed the milling of flour, which, if combined with water, could be turned into dough easily baked near or in a fire, thus eliminating the need for a ceramic cooking pot. Others have suggested that the large amount of shellfish remains associated with early ceramic sites points to cooking solutions for foods not easily baked or roasted on an open fire; boiling them in a pot was a far better approach (Lü 2010) and is in fact common among other early ceramic cultures, namely those found in Japan (Craig et al. 2013). The recent early pottery site of **Houtaomuga** in Jilin Province, North China (~11.5 KYA), exhibits extensive exploitation of marine resources, possibly practiced by seasonal sedentary forager groups making the most of available aquatic animals (Wang & Sebillaud 2019).

Yet there are certainly other ways to boil liquids. Thousands of fragments of cracked rock found at the later phases of Shuidonggou site #12 (~10.5 KYA), where no ceramics existed, indicate the importance of indirect stone boiling. This technique involves heating the rocks in a fire and then placing them in liquid, in cooking implements made of animal skin or hide (Gao et al. 2014). What was cooked here is less clear, but remains of buffalo, deer, birds, rabbits, rodents, antelopes (Przewalski's gazelle), boar and equids were discovered at the site, all of which could have been roasted and not boiled, of course. Environmental reconstructions suggest a mixed savanna-like surrounding with marsh plants at the time of occupation, likely including roots, fruits and grasses that would have benefited from boiling. An additional suggestion, but one that is quite hard to assess, is that water was boiled to kill harmful pathogens and make it safe to drink (Yi et al. 2021b).

Brian Hayden has made the argument that ceramics, much like the development of agriculture, were connected to a desire by would-be aggrandizers to utilize a novel technology in order to climb the social ladder (see Section 3). New and presumably desirable food and drink could be produced with ceramics and then feasted upon, thus garnering prestige and higher standing for those able to create and utilize ceramic technologies (Hayden 2009). Some have postulated that early ceramics may have been used to extract precious substances (specifically fat) from animal bones, possibly during times of food stress (Elston et al. 2011; Wu et al. 2012). One can effectively use woven baskets or animal intestines and skin to boil liquid with hot stones, but prolonged simmering, required for the extraction of bone grease, would be challenging. A recent study has argued that, given the low temperatures of the hearths associated with the earliest ceramics at Yuchanyan and the fragmented cervid bones found with them, cooking bone soup might have been what early ceramics were used for (Patania & Jaffe 2021). Prolonged simmering is best achieved at low temperatures – staying around 100° C is ideal for a low rolling boil. The inhabitants of Yuchanyan exhibited a deep understanding of pyrotechnology in the way they organized their fires and cooked food in pots over them. Fire features and hardened clay surfaces were found in a central part of the cave. They were repeatedly cleaned and reused, possibly in a seasonal manner, for many years (Patania et al. 2019).

If indeed early ceramics were used to make bone soup and render grease, this was a multistage and extended process, one would-be social climbers would find nearly impossible to accomplish on their own, regardless of how committed they were. Fires needed to be tended for hours, water added periodically to replenish evaporated liquid, and the fire would have required careful feeding and watching so as not to overheat the pot. The results of this labor (an intensive and time-consuming activity) would have been enjoyed, probably by the entire group, on the move (grease can congeal into nice packages of portable protein and fat), or even during feasts, bringing members of the groups further together after the completion of the arduous task (Patania & Jaffe 2021).

Food in the Early Holocene: The Slow Process toward Farming

At the start of the Holocene era, communities were using microliths, ceramics and grinding tools in a diverse manner (Figure 3). Near modern-day Beijing, at the site of **Donghulin** (9000–7000 BCE), pits, graves and even hearths were found alongside several dozen grinding stones and ceramic vessels. Grinding stones were used to process acorns or millet, possibly under the very initial stages of cultivation (Yang et al. 2012). Ornate sickle blades show the increased importance of grain, probably still wild, consumed alongside deer, acorns and

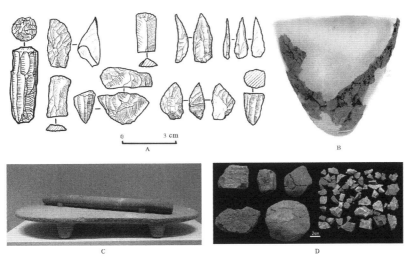

Figure 3 A. Microliths of the Xiachuan culture (after Shelach 2015, 52).
B. Early Neolithic pottery from Yuchanyan (photo credit: Professor Fu Xianguo). C. Stone quern and roller of the Peiligang culture, Peiligang site (photo credit: Rong Fan). D. Cracked rock fragments unearthed from Shuidonggou Locality 12 (Photo courtesy of Professor Gao Xing)

berries (Zhao et al. 2020). Millet and acorns were important further south as well. **Nanzhuangtou** in Hebei (~9000–6500 BCE) yielded some of the earliest evidence for domesticated dogs (*Canis familiaris*), alongside a majority of hunted deer (Hebei et al. 2010; Yuan & Li 2010). According to Yang and colleagues (2012), millet was processed with grinding stones and dogs at the site were also fed with millet (Hou et al. 2021).

While the ceramics at Nanzhuangtou and Donghulin were found alongside flaked tools, the Nihewan basin site of **Houtouliang** (~8500 BCE) exhibited a large number of sophisticated bladelets and finely retouched points (Zhang et al. 2010). The pottery here is flat bottomed, unlike the rounded pots found elsewhere, leading some to suggest that pottery at Houtouliang would have been used for storage rather than cooking (Lü 2010) – though more study of the vessels themselves is required to assess this claim. At **Lijiagou**, overlooking a bank of the Yellow River Valley in Henan Province (~8500 BCE), early stone tools were core-and-flake assemblages that slowly gave way to a microblade industry. These were found alongside the possible remains of huts, grinding stones and coarse ceramic vessels. The faunal assemblage is dominated by deer, wild boar and bovines and small mammals, mostly rabbit and rodents, and even occasional ostrich eggs (Wang et al. 2015).

In the south, in the lower Yangzi reaches of Zhejiang Province, at the **Shangshan** site (~8000–6200 BCE), there is some evidence to suggest rice cultivation and the continued reliance on acorns in local diets (Huan et al. 2021). Combined use and wear and chemical residue analysis of ceramic vessels and grinding stones suggests that rice was minimally processed at Shangshan before consumption (Zuo et al. 2017). Indeed, the combination of grinding stones and ceramic vessels may have been used together to process acorns and not rice, as acorns are quite toxic. Initially, they were ground into meal, then leached with water in open basins, cooked in constricted jars and, finally, served in plates as porridge or soup (Wang & Jiang 2022).

Bianbiandong (8000 BCE) is a cave site in Shandong that has preserved pottery and possible dog bones at the southeast region of the Yellow River Basin. Here, hunters focused on wild animals such as deer (90 percent), but were not averse to consuming, wild boars, birds and freshwater mollusks. These were discovered alongside millets, nuts and wild fruits such as apricot, peach, grapes and berries (Sun et al. 2014). Over the following two millennia, human societies began to move out of caves onto the alluvial plains and consumed more pork, as well as a variety of other plants and animals. Since there is little evidence for environmental changes over this time period, some argue that a desire to retain sedentary lifeways would have required these groups to diversify their food sources so as to be able to remain fixed year-round (Song et al. 2019c).

- - - - - -

At the end of the Late Glacial period and the beginning of the warmer Holocene era, communities across the ancient landscape were experimenting (some would even say playing) with novel ways of obtaining and preparing food. Well before the advent of farming lifeways, the topic of the next section, human societies in Ancient China had sophisticated stone tools – microliths – for hunting a wide range of animals and harvesting a multitude of plants. Ground stone tools, mortars and grinding stones provided specialized implements for dehusking and grinding roots, tubers, nuts and seeds. Ceramic cooking vessels offered control over the same fire that had been used for hundreds of thousands of years to roast and bake food. Now humans could boil, simmer, braise, steam and stew old ingredients in new ways. Hunter-gatherer groups continued to broaden their diets and also began, slowly, to rely more heavily on the gathered grains and nuts for daily sustenance. Through their continual selection, some of these plants would eventually transform and rely more heavily on humans for their survival as well. These initial cultivation efforts lasted several millennia and should not be seen as following a well-thought-out strategy to domesticate wild plant and animals. Humans did, however, more actively manage their ecological settings and, as they did, they further deepened their connection to specific locations.

3 The Rise and Development of Agricultural Societies

Cultivating Plants and Animals

The transition to agriculture is one of the most important changes in humanity's past, and China is one of only a handful of regions where plants and animals were domesticated. Agriculture impacted far more than just how humans acquired their food; it changed their social organizations and political structures, fueling in some cases the rise of inequality and, perhaps most significantly, it allowed the continual development of social complexity. As we will see, this was not an event-like revolution, but a prolonged process of experimentation, false starts and play that resulted in a wide range of sociopolitical outcomes (Graeber & Wengrow 2021).

Definitions of agriculture further complicate its study (for a China-specific overview, see Shelach 2015, chapter 3). Agriculture is widely understood as a socioeconomic system where humans rely on the processing of domesticated plants and animals for sustenance, rather than the hunting and gathering of wild species. Plants and animals undergo phenotypic and genetic changes during domestication that separate them from their wild ancestors – for example, floppy ears and smaller brains in animals, and increased fruit size and non-shattering spikelet in plants. Once domesticated, many plants and animals are unable to propagate without the aid of humans. A main aspect of the early agriculture debate is one of scale and relates to two main elements (see classic overviews in Price & Bar-Yosef 2011): 1) The stage of the domestication process one deems exemplary of agriculture – that is, is domestication acknowledged during initial stages, even before morphological changes took place, or only when the final transition has occurred and fully domesticated, nearly modern-day specimens are found? 2) The centrality of domesticated species in a group's diet – that is, does the majority of consumed food need to be domesticated, or is the consumption of a single domesticate enough to push a society into the agriculture pile?

These are important questions, but ones we cannot get bogged down by. What is crucial is to appreciate the mental change domestication brings about in human societies. The intensive cultivation of plants would have disrupted their natural growing habitats and ability to self-propagate. Even if harvesting and processing continued as before, domesticated plants demanded careful considerations of the fields they were planted in, which could result over time in increased seasonal sedentism. The raising of farm animals demanded great changes as well. As Price (2021 p. 21) notes: "These adaptations pushed humans to reconsider their relationships with animals, initiating a revolutionary cultural transformation that flipped the logic of hunting on its head: people shifted from a focus on obtaining meat from dead animals to acquiring and maintaining live ones."

Plants

Archaeological research over the past several decades has uncovered the types of animals and plants domesticated in China, where and when they were domesticated and their connection to previous gatherer-hunter economies (see overviews in Crawford 2017; Liu & Ma 2017; Matuzevičiūtė & Liu 2021). In China and elsewhere, staple grains are the focus of many studies, as they are often viewed as the central aspect of farming economies, providing a majority of the calories as well as necessitating a more sedentary lifestyle. A marked divide is seen between northern China, where millet was arguably the most important staple crop, and the south, where it was rice. Both broomcorn (*Panicum miliaceum*) and foxtail (*Setaria italica*) millets were cultivated intensively in the Loess Plateau to the north of the Yellow River Valley by at least 7000 BCE (Barton et al. 2009; Stevens et al. 2021; Yang et al. 2012). Rice (*Oryza sativa*) was extensively gathered and cultivated around 8000 BCE in the Yangzi River Valley. Both grains underwent a prolonged selection process for thousands of years, continually evolving desired traits, such as non-shattering spikelet and increased grain size (Zheng et al. 2016). These important crops began to spread from their initial centers of cultivation around 7000 BCE and prompted mixed economic strategies for growing rice and millet in Central and eastern China (Bestel et al. 2018; Jin et al. 2014; Weisskopf et al. 2015). Further west, in modern-day Qinghai, Gansu, Sichuan and Yunnan, millets and rice, as well as other domesticates, arrived several millennia later and continued to undergo selective cultivation (Dal Martello 2022; d'Alpoim Guedes 2011; d'Alpoim Guedes et al. 2014; Yang et al. 2018a).

With the growing importance of archaeobotanical protocols for soil sifting and flotation, and the incorporation of new analytical tools, such as residue and starch grain analysis, have revealed the importance of other grains: buckwheat (*Fagopyrum esculentum* and *F. tataricum*), for example, may have been domesticated in China as early as ~3500 BCE, but this remains debatable (Hunt et al. 2018). Soy beans (*Glycine max*) have been identified in the Early Neolithic era though domesticated later – its precise dating remains controversial with some studies pushing its domestication into the Bronze Age (Lee et al. 2011). Roots and tubers (including varieties of yams, gourds and lotus) were continually utilized throughout the Neolithic era and underwent a slow process of domestication (Stevens & Fuller 2017; Zhao 2011). More recently still, the importance of nuts, including acorns, walnuts (*Juglans mandshurica*) and hazelnuts (*Corylus* spp.); beans and legumes, including red bean and azuki (*Vigna angularis*); as well as fruit, such as apricot (*Prunus armeniaca*), jujube (*Ziziphus jujube*), peach (*Prunus. persica*) and plum (*Prunus simonii*), have been highlighted in gatherer-hunter diets. These plants and others underwent cultivation during the Early Neolithic era and were eventually domesticated only during the late third millennium BCE (Crawford 2017; Fuller & Stevens 2019; Shen & Li 2021; Zhang et al. 2018; Zheng et al. 2014).

Animals

Like plants, the timing and pace of animal domestication is an ongoing topic of research. It is by now well established that wolves (*Canis lupus*) were the earliest animals to have been domesticated, with some suggesting an endemic process from local populations, possibly during the late Pleistocene (Frantz et al. 2016; Larson et al. 2012). Dogs were food, but were an important component in obtaining food as well – they may have provided the means to hunt more dangerous animals such as wild boar (Price 2021). Dogs were consumed throughout the Neolithic era and into the Bronze Age, but always in small amounts (Yuan et al. 2008). Pigs were domesticated independently in China, perhaps as early as the seventh millennium BCE and in more than one location (Cucchi et al. 2011; Dong & Yuan 2020; Lander et al. 2020; Larson et al. 2010; Price & Hongo 2019).

Initially, pigs and dogs were thought to have been the only two domesticated animals available to humans in Ancient China, and together with millet and rice were seen as staples that enabled the long transition to agricultural lifeways. Recently, some have made the argument that chickens (*Gallus gallus domesticus*) were first domesticated in North China quite early, around 10 KYA (Xiang et al. 2014). These early dates remain quite controversial, however, with most proposing the late second millennium BCE or the Shang dynasty for large-scale poultry farming (Eda et al. 2016). Cattle domestication is still a matter of vigorous debate, and a number of wild specimens are implicated in the process: wild aurochs, domesticated taurine cattle (*Bos taurus*), domesticated zebu (*Bos indicus*), wild and domesticated yak (*Bos Mutus, Bos grunniens*), as well as wild and domesticated water buffalo (*Bubalus mephistopheles, Bubalus bubalis*) (Chen et al. 2018; Lu et al. 2017). Wild cattle were hunted in mass in Northwest China as early as 3500 BCE (Cai et al. 2018), but Brunson et al. (2020) have cautioned against viewing pre-2500 BCE cattle as domesticated. The bones of wild water buffalo, hunted and consumed in Neolithic sites of the Lower Yangzi, were supposedly used to fashion hafted digging tools (Xie 2018) and, if true, would point to the complex relationship farmers had with their environments: hunting wild animals for meat and using their bones to make tools to grow domesticated crops. Other important livestock animals, sheep, goat (collectively caprines) and horses were introduced into China sometime in the fourth or third millennium BCE (see Section 4).

These six domesticates – cattle, horse, sheep, goat, pig, dog and chicken – are thought to have been the primary livestock breeds during historical and imperial China. As such, they are an important part of zooarchaeological research efforts (Yuan & Dong 2018). Other domesticated animals were geese (*Anser*) in the lower Yangzi region around 5000 BCE (Eda et al. 2022), a time when pheasant (*Phasianus colchicus*) exploitation was underway in the north (Barton et al. 2020). Rodents, rabbits and birds are often found in and around archaeological sites, though it is hard to know if they were eaten by humans or lived around them and consumed the foods produced by humans (mostly their garbage). When bone and stone tools, traps or nets are found, as well as filleting cut marks on the bones themselves, they can be more readily assumed to have been eaten (Sheng et al. 2020).

Domestication and the Development of Sedentary Lifeways (~7000–5000 BCE)

The transition to fully fledged agricultural lifeways was a slow process. It would take several millennia until societies would fully rely on domesticated plants and animals as exclusive food sources. The recent discovery of carp bones demonstrates the complex commensal pathway of early agriculture as communities raised fish in flooded rice plots (Nakajima et al. 2019). The continued intensification of cultivation and food-producing strategies was coupled with increased evidence for sedentary lifestyles (Figure 4). Communities across Ancient China exhibited marked sophistication in tool production, while the diversity of economic strategies reflected regional adaptations as well as the evolution of food preferences and culinary systems.

The Central Yellow River Valley – The **Peiligang/Cishan culture** (~7000–5000 BCE) has played a central role in discussions on the transition to agriculture. To date, hundreds of sites have been documented, though far fewer have been excavated. Residential areas were often surrounded by ditches enclosing several houses and pits for storage and waste. While domesticated pigs, dogs and millet were cultivated, people continued to hunt and fish a large variety of wild animals, such as boar, hare and turtles, but mostly deer that were hunted year-round (Zhu 2013). Wild plant gathering also remained important and included a variety of tubers, nuts and fruits (Bestel et al. 2018). Analysis of stone tools such as sickles and denticules revealed a range of plants processed by these tools, wild grasses together with millet and rice (Fullagar et al. 2021). In fact, grinding stones, abundantly found at these sites, may not have been used to process much millet, but, as

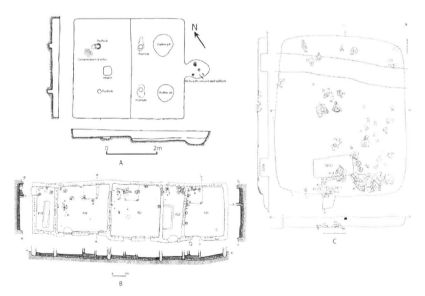

Figure 4 Neolithic houses (A: House F6 from the Zhaobaogou site, after Shelach 2015: 76; B. House 19–23 from the Yuchisi site, after CASS 2001: 65; C. F301 from the Xihe site, after Shandong and Chengziya 2012: 75)

in earlier periods, acorns (Liu et al. 2010). This may point to how these plants were prepared; millet was boiled, while acorns were ground to flour.

The site of **Jiahu** (7000–5000 BCE) has yielded some of the earliest culti-vated rice remains, though they may not have been a large part of the diet. Here too hunting, fishing and the gathering of wild resources, grapes (*Vitis spp.*), soy and tubers, remained important (Zhang et al. 2018; Zhao 2010) alongside the raising of domesticated pigs (Cucchi et al. 2011). The Jiahu site provides an exceptional view into the social life of an early farming village. Musical instruments accompanied early evidence for alcohol consumption though little evidence for social ranking can be seen (Zhang & Hung 2013). Processing rice into flour was accomplished using a dry grinding technique conducive to the preparation of certain foods, such as doughs, and extended the shelf life of stored goods (Li et al. 2019a).

Central China, the *Yangzi River Basin* – A marked degree of site planning is exhibited at **Pengtoushan** and **Bashidang** (of the Pengtoushan culture ~7500–6000 BCE), where agricultural needs were of prime concern. The sites were situated on the edges of the alluvial plain and along loess terraces, ideal for the management and watering of crops, and large numbers of specialized stone tools for working the fields were found. Both sites yielded large numbers of rice grains, possibly cultivated, though the initially beneficial geographic setting may have turned determinantal once the groundwater table began to rise, ostensibly forcing the local population to abandon rice farming and rely more heavily on foraging at Bashidang (Liu et al. 2017b). Indeed, both sites yielded large amounts of wild acorns, Job's tears (*Coix lacryma-jobi*) and domesticated dogs alongside pigs, even as various taxa of wild animals continued to dominate the assemblages (Yuan et al. 2008).

In the Lower (Eastern) Yangzi Basin, the wet and hot climate is more conducive to rice agriculture and early evidence for its cultivation is found at the site of Shangshan ~8500 BCE (Zuo et al. 2017), more fully domesticated later at Tianluoshan (~7000–5000 BCE) (Fuller et al. 2009). The inhabitants of **Kuahuqiao** (~6000–5000 BCE), in Zhejiang Province, continued to cultivate their available food sources while expertly adapting to their environmental conditions. The houses here were constructed of wood, the floors raised above the marshy surface, most likely to prevent flooding and water damage. Rice may not have been an important crop at this site where acorns, wild foxnuts (*Euryale ferox*) and water caltrop (*Trapa natans*) were widely consumed. Ceramic vessels were used mainly to boil starchy plants (Shoda et al. 2018) and large square-shaped storage pits were lined with wooden beams to protect crops. Interestingly, these pits were found filled with large quantities of acorns, not rice (Jiang 2013). Domesticated pigs and dogs were reared, but the variety of wild animal species is quite astounding: everything from shellfish, dolphins (*Delphinidae*), deer, water buffalo, swan (*Cygnus* sp.) and even tiger, was consumed. Settling at the ecotone between forests, wetland swaps and the sea coast, the area's inhabitants were able to maintain sedentary lifestyles to consume a broad diet year-round (Pan et al. 2017). Nutrient extraction was maximized and bones of larger animals were broken up, indicating bone marrow consumption. Cut marks on bone indicate high-level butchery skills were needed to prepare specific dishes. These were matched by a variety of steamers and large cauldrons for boiling and simmering, alongside a wide range of elaborate serving dishes (Jiang 2013).

Northeastern China – The harsh winters and hot dry summers of North China required different subsistence strategies. The **Xiaohexi culture** (~6500–5700 BCE) is characterized by short-lived and small-sized communities that invested less in their permanent structures. Pig rearing and millet cultivation, possibly in the early stages of domestication, are well attested in the region during this time, but were complemented by foraging for wild grasses, seeds and tubers (Stevens et al. 2021). Hunting continued to be important, with many sites yielding near 50 percent deer, even as pigs were gaining importance (Tu et al. 2022). In fact, while the transition to sedentary lifeways in this region was rather fast in comparison to other regions in China, the transition to fully fledged agricultural lifeways may have been a more prolonged process (Shelach-Lavi et al. 2019). Recent excavations at **Chahai** suggest that early stages of the transition to sedentism, experimentation and low-level food production may have been a communal effort, though households were independent domestic units. Houses at Chahai were enclosed spaces, each boasted its own hearth, and many contained implements for preparing and cooking food. All houses yielded tools to prepare and consume food, their number positively correlated with house size and likely the number of inhabitants who would have resided in them (Tu et al. 2022). Even as food was cooked in the privacy of one's home, some foodstuffs may have been shared as storage pits are found between houses. Contributing to intercommunity cohesion were feasts, as evidenced by waste pits abundant with pottery and burnt pig bones found in the central square (Tu et al. 2022).

Over time, sedentism became more central throughout the region but collectivism decreased. Sites of the **Xinglongwa** (~6200–5200 BCE) and **Zhaobaogou** (5200–4500 BCE) **cultures** grew in size and exhibited higher levels of site planning as they were now home to several hundred individuals (Shelach 2006). Households at the eponymous sites of Xinglongwa and later Zhaobaogou continued to be the central loci of food production and consumption, but most houses kept internal storage implements, including dug-in pits or large vessels, some able to hold ~30 L of grain – enough to support one individual for several months. Houses were built in neat rows, doors facing the same direction, and included large stone tools, possibly for agricultural use, indicating that farming, not just eating, was undertaken at the household level as well (Shelach 2006). Unlike Chahai, no central plazas are found either hinting at the individualistic nature that began to take hold over these communities, once more developed agriculture economies were formed.

The Lower Reaches of the Yellow River – In the Far East, Shandong Province, societies during the **Houli culture** period (~6500–5500 BCE) chose to build their homes on terraces alongside riverbanks and subsisted on a varied diet consisting of both domesticated millet and rice. Stable isotope analysis shows that disparate rates of millet and rice were eaten at different Houli sites and that neither one of these crops may have contributed more than one-fourth of all calories consumed. Even people of the same community ate different foods. At **Yuezhang** and **Xihe**, rice remains were found concentrated in a small number of locations (both prior to and after processing), and more freely shared at others like Yuezhuang (Jin et al. 2014). Determining whether this resulted from a preference for certain foods or limited access to otherwise desirable grains is challenging. At the same time, while all sites raised domesticated pigs, they also consumed a wide variety of animal and fish species. Here again sites display different tastes: the community at Xihe hunted but preferred fish (Song et al., 2021), the residents of Yuezhuang combined hunted deer with fish, and at **Zhangmatun** and **Xiaojingshan** people enjoyed their shellfish (Wu, 2019). Certain sites reveal a higher abundance of specialized tools, such as stone hammer *chui* balls, potentially used for processing nuts. However, nearly all sites utilized grinding tools and large round-bottomed *fu* cauldrons, used to boil and stew various ingredients. Most all Houli houses are big, large enough to accommodate at least ten people, and the fact that some include more than one hearth indicates that cooking and feeding the extended family or guests was quite important.

Agricultural Catalysts or Agricultural Outcomes: Ceramics and Alcohol

The transition to agriculture in China was evidently a prolonged process. The domestication of plants and animals, which took several hundred, if not thousands, of years, resulted in these species becoming just one additional component in a diverse selection of wild foods. This realization, which is in no way unique to China, has effectively questioned prime mover explanations for the shift from mobile hunter-gatherer groups to sedentary farming communities. If agriculture was a deliberate action taken to cope with impending hunger due to population expansion, the delayed returns on investment is problematic. (An R&D department promising to deliver the finished product sometime in the next millennia would be axed on the spot.) Unexpected environmental stress that would have required radical economic changes seems less likely as well, since climatic records show large regional differences in conditions and rapidity of environmental changes. This climatic variability also challenges models that find optimal environmental conditions to have allowed affluent societies to experiment with animal and plant cultivation. Similarly, the social model appears unlikely since it also necessitates a certain level of environmental predictability, enabling potential aggrandizers to cultivate and accumulate desirable foods, with which to gain prestige within their community. Therefore, stress, whether caused by population or environmental factors, is less than ideal for such endeavors. Further still, the long transition to agriculture does not seem to have been accompanied, at least not during its earlier phases, with the development of deep social inequality. (See Shelach, 2015, chapter 3, for an overview of these models in China. For new approaches and definitions for domestication, see, for example, Allaby et al. 2022; Bogaard et al. 2021; Spengler 2020; Zeder 2015.)

At the same time aspects of these models ring true. Societies might have faced changing climates at the onset of the warmer (on average) Holocene epoch. When dealing with stress, be it population pressure or resources scarcity, even plants in their early stages of cultivation could provide that extra level of food security, just enough to make the difference between starving and surviving (Price & Bar-Yosef 2011). Locational analysis of early farming communities across China reveals that sites were concentrated to some extent up on the hilly flanks along alluvial fans and lake edges where maximum productivity could be achieved through intensive cultivation – a trend similar to that seen at other parts of the world (Liu et al. 2019b). In North China, the advent of sedentism and cultivation appears to have coincided with wetter conditions than those experienced before in the region (Shelach et al. 2019).

Brian Hayden's notion that agriculture was motivated by the desire to obtain valuable foodstuffs, enabling potential aggrandizers to host feasts and gain favor, might hold some merit as well; almost as soon as they underwent cultivation, plants (grains mostly) were fermented, malted, mashed and brewed to create alcoholic beverages. Chemical analysis of ceramic vessels alongside starch granules and phytoliths point to the production and consumption of alcohol as early as 7000 BCE, made of different mixtures of rice, millet, Job's tears, beans, yams, roots, honey, fruits and more (Liu et al. 2019a; McGovern et al. 2004; Wang et al. 2021). Grains (millet chief among them) were a favorite and common base for alcohol production; their fermentation may have involved a number of different processes and starters, including human saliva or sprouted, malted or moldy grains left to develop yeast, fungi and bacteria (Liu 2021).

Even if not a major catalyst in the agricultural transition, alcohol was an undeniably important outcome of domestication. Some argue that the variety of ceramic types seen quite early during the Neolithic era may have been connected to the production and consumption of alcoholic beverages, and a desire for better brewing results and the impetus for continued ceramic development (Liu 2021; Liu et al. 2019a). The large quantity and quality of pottery vessels found at Neolithic sites (Figure 5) is far greater than the earlier, simple, low-fired forms of the earliest ceramics.

Large containers for storing dry goods and liquids, elaborate cooking pots and sets of serving dishes with colorful decorations and intricate designs are found in nearly every household now. Notable regional differences can be seen and are represented in the styles and decorations as well as in their shapes and size. A brief examination of the shapes and types of vessels clearly demonstrates the diversity in which food was prepared and served. Meals were prepared in *li* cooking tripods at some communities, their three-legged design allowing them to be elevated over a fire, while vessels constructed with a rounded bottom, like *fu*,

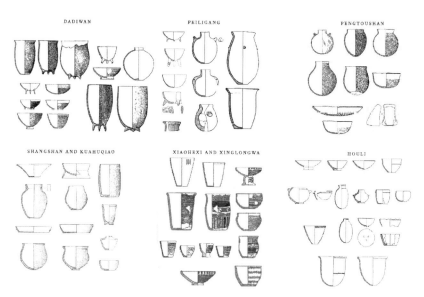

Figure 5 Comparison of ceramic vessels from Dadiwan (after CASS 2010, 116, 118 5), Peiligang (after Henan First Team CASS et al. 2020, 532, 533, 535, 537, 538), Pengtoushan (after Wang and Qu 2018, 73), Shangshan and Kuahuqiao (after Sun 2016, 99, 103; Xu and Chen 2019,170) Xiaohexi and Xinglongwa (after Gao 2021: 28–30; Shelach 2015, 90), Houli (after Lu 2022: 100)

were placed directly in the hot coals. Heat exposure and control is but one culinary aspect here; the size of both cooking and storing vessels, *guan* and *weng* further indicates growing concerns with eating party size and the need to prepare enough food and serve it in the appropriate dishes and tableware. Ecological settings had a pivotal role in shaping local diets, but above all, it seems that culinary preferences and community-specific foodways were increasingly influencing what people consumed and how they prepared their meals.

4 Into the Middle Neolithic Era (5000–3000 BCE): Food for New Thoughts

Once we move into the fifth millennium BCE, or the Middle Neolithic era, we begin to encounter societies growing and raising fully domesticated plants and animals and residing in villages not unlike those of traditional farming communities. The process of cereal domestication was nearly complete around this time, millet dominating the Yellow River Valley and rice the Yangzi, but in many communities, both were integrated into a single agricultural system (Stevens & Fuller 2017). Hunting and gathering were no longer vital nor were they abandoned, and agriculture, now a focal part of the economy, provided the backdrop for these societies to prosper in new ways – even as venison and wild rice remained on the menu. It is during this time that major social changes were underway and would reach unprecedented quantitative leaps in the third and second millennia BCE (Section 5). Sites were larger, more numerous and more densely packed than those of the Early Neolithic era. Feeding growing populations was but one concern; making sure people had enough to eat *and* get along in these large sites was another challenge entirely. Existing social and political systems would have required at least some modification to accommodate new settlement organizations. Economic activities varied between communities but inequality, where it existed, was not as pronounced as one might expect, even when power was centralized. Throughout the ancient landscape, communities incorporated a blend of agriculture, hunting, and gathering to different extents while evolving their distinct regional-specific styles, social practices, political systems and, naturally, foodways. In this section, I focus on fewer sites but offer a more comprehensive examination of their remains to better assess their significance in terms of foodways.

Agricultural Communities in the Middle Neolithic Era (~5000–3000 BCE)

In the Lower Yangzi region, the **Hemudu** site (~5000–3000 BCE) provides excellent evidence on developed Neolithic lifeways. Like Kuahuqiao, the marshy lands prevented the decay of wooden elements at the site, and its pole-raised wooden houses were spread out across several hectares (Song 2013). Foraging continued to be important; acorns and chestnuts were prevalent, but Hemudu yielded an absolutely astounding amount of rice remains (some estimate 20 tons!), together with evidence for rice paddy fields and sophisticated stone, bone and wooden agricultural elements (Xie et al. 2017). At the same time, more than sixty animal species were found at the site: alongside domesticated pigs and dogs (and possibly water buffalo) were numerous deer, elephants (*Elephas maximus*), wild boar and panthers (*Panthera*). Aquatic water fowl included crane, goose and even eagle (*Aquila clanga*), and plentiful marine resources of alligator (*Alligator sinensis*), several species of turtle (e.g., *Amyda sinensis* and *Chelonia mydas*), crab and mollusks, as well as many fish (Song 2013). Pottery variation and style was impressive. Large *fu* cauldrons and *yan* steamers cooked food and elaborate serving vessels, many with glossy black finishes and intricate geometric and zoomorphic designs, presented their contents. Residue analysis of ceramic *bo* bowls suggest that they may have contained a mix of acorns and bone – perhaps crushed into a powder. Only a few bowls have been analyzed, but as they are found only in children's graves, this finding might reflect a particular dietary aspect of early life at Hemudu (Ge et al. 2021).

In the Yellow River Valley region, the **Yangshao** culture period (circa 5000–3000) is one marked with considerable change. Social differentiation, religious beliefs, new crafts, production advances and techniques can be seen with the manipulation of jade, while ceramic workshops reached unprecedented levels of sophistication and elaboration (Liu & Chen 2012, chapter 6; Shelach 2015, chapter 4). **Jiangzhai,** arguably one of the best excavated and extensively published of any Neolithic sites, provides a truly exceptional view on the development of food and society during this time. A roughly 2 ha site in size, it features structures built around a large open plaza. The whole site, home to several hundred people, was encircled with a deep trench; the cemetery was found outside it. Jiangzhai has been the focus of many studies engaged with the nature of social hierarchy and incipient inequality at the site. Some view the community as consisting of several lineages or families, each with its respective leader, as evidenced by five distinct clusters of smaller houses around a central larger one, while others perceive these clusters as communal gathering structures (see Lee 2007).

In their work, Peterson and Shelach (2012) offer valuable insights into the food and foodways at Jiangzhai. They concentrate on grain storage and intra-community sharing practices, as well as the preparation and consumption of meals, making their analysis particularly noteworthy. While the central plaza, presumably communal ground, was where animals (pigs mostly) were penned, grain storage pits were connected to individual households, indicating more restricted sharing of grain. They postulate that if all the pits found at the site (well over 100) were filled, the community would have had enough stored grain to sustain them for an entire year. Different households, however, maintained pits of varying sizes that did not corelate with house size, possibly a choice related to investment in agricultural production. I would further suggest that this was, perhaps, a product of household risk management strategies. As Hastorf and Foxhall (2017) have argued, what constitutes a risk-averse practice – that is, the amount of storage people feel they need for a rainy (or dry) day – depends upon cultural standards. This certainly was the case in their comparative study of Inca and ancient Athenian societies. Did food security mean different things for different households at Jiangzhai? Meat may have alleviated risk and food security concerns as well, as its consumption was unequally distributed across the site. Some areas included more bones than others, especially interesting when we remember that animal pens are found in the communal plaza area – either livestock was raised communally or individual households kept their own animals in a shared pen. The five sectors also differed in terms of their artifact assemblages, with several sectors exhibiting higher proportions of agricultural implements for ploughing, sowing, harvesting and processing, while others included more hunting tools. Curiously, the area with the highest proportion of agricultural related tools also had the least amount of storage implements in it and the lowest numbers of animal bones. Ceramic vessels used to serve and present food were, unsurprisingly, found in equal numbers among the different sectors, but were unequally distributed among the houses of the different sectors. Inviting neighbors to dinner seems to have been more important for some at Jiangzhai and possibly less so for others.

While some scholars argue that Yangshao-period communities would have cooperatively processed crops in bulk on a communal basis (Song et al. 2019a; Weisskopf et al. 2015), other societies in the northern regions may have organized their agricultural systems in a bimodal fashion. In this system, one group engaged in more intensive farming, while another provided different services in return. The **Hongshan** culture (~4500–3000 BCE) in Liaoning and Inner Mongolia subsisted on farmed millet, domesticated pigs and hunted animals. Hongshan is best known for elaborate graves, containing exquisite jades, and impressive ceremonial structures built out of stone, centered, some suggest, around a female goddess of healing. The **Niuheliang** ceremonial center, often referred to as the core zone of the Hongshan culture, is a dense agglomeration of platforms, graves, mounds and small residential communities spanning several dozen square kilometers. Regional surveys have noted that many Hongshan sites were small, likely single farmsteads, though most of the population was concentrated in villages inhabited by several hundred individuals (Drennan et al. 2017).

The communities near the ceremonial architectural features were not situated on prime agricultural lands (where most settlements are indeed found during subsequent periods), promoting some to suggest that these communities were supported by the visiting pilgrims to whom they provided services in return. Ran (2022) has recently shown that some nearby communities practiced food production at higher levels than those at Niuheliang. At one such community, those households that displayed the highest amounts of food production tools were also those that exhibited the highest amount of decorated serving ware. Food may have been sent to the ceremonial centers, but it was also used to host guests from the immediate community.

Seeds of Inequality in the Late Neolithic Era: Alcohol and Meat for the Dead and the Living

Pigs had been living alongside humans in China for thousands of years, but it was only after the fifth millennium BCE that they began to play a significant role in human diets. In fact, they would become a dominant food source during the second millennium BCE, and only in some regions (Lander et al. 2020; Pan and Yuan 2018; Yuan 1999; Yuan et al. 2008). The Middle Yellow River Region experienced wider dependence on cultivated pigs earlier on (Ma 2005). The site of **Dadiwan** in Gansu (~6000–3000 BCE) provides evidence for these developments as it was continually inhabited throughout the Neolithic era. What started out as a small site of hunter-gatherers who experimented with millet cultivation grew into a huge 50 ha site by the Late Yangshao period. Early on, inhabitants subsisted on wild plants and deer, but over time millet become more central to the diet, as well as that of their dogs and pigs who were probably fed with table scraps (Barton et al. 2009). Raising pigs for consumption was a goal unto itself, but it facilitated agricultural intensification as well. Pigs were nourished with millet, including grains, stems and other by-products. Their manure served as a valuable fertilizer for the fields, enhancing soil fertility and promoting the cultivation of additional millet. This, in turn, enabled the sustenance of an expanding pig population, creating a continuous cycle of resource utilization (Yang et al. 2022).

The role pigs played in society appears to have changed during this time as well: from ritually significant animals found in graves early in the Neolithic era to important aspects of communal consumption. Younger piglets were favored in these social gatherings whereas older pigs were often placed in graves (Luo 2012). In fact, this is also when some scholars believe competitive feasting would have played an important role. Feasting, consuming large amounts of alcohol and food (often meat), has many social functions, chiefly bringing people together. Feasts are of course quite political and those who organize a feast hope to gain prestige and improve their rank and standing (Bray 2003; Dietler & Hayden 2001; Smith 2015). Often, holding great feasts is the main way to gain power and to maintain it. At other times it is a way to reaffirm existing social relationships or to welcome new members into a community (and see Twiss 2019, chapter 5, for an overview on feasts and feasting in archaeology). Whatever the occasion, pork and alcohol would have been a prodigious combination for tasty gatherings.

The expansion of Dadiwan during the Late Neolithic era included the construction of a number of large structures; the largest, which measured more than 300 square meters, was situated on an elevated platform with a large hearth at its center and a well-paved floor. The purpose of these large structures remains ambiguous, as they could either signify elite buildings or serve as the public centers for communal life, where ritual feasts or ceremonies were held. Levels of inequality seem to have increased during this time, as seen in burial differentiation, at the same time when new evidence points to growth in conspicuous consumption and far-off trade across Ancient China: the movement of unique, scarce and labor-intensive resources (e.g., cinnabar, jade, ivory) and fine craft goods, increased in importance throughout the Neolithic era, but during this earlier period, foodstuffs, domesticated plants and animals were circulated more widely (Hua et al. 2020; e.g., Lee et al. 2007; Wang et al. 2019). Li Liu (2021) suggests that alcohol consumption held a dual function at this period of population increase and growing social differentiation. Feasting and drinking would have been a way to maintain social cohesion and thus prevent potential splintering of the community, and, additionally, help maintain interregional ties. Alcoholic beverages might have been consumed communally, sipped through straws from shared basins, some of them imported themselves, at events where it is not unlikely that foreign gifts were distributed, dancing was performed and good food was eaten.

The late Yangshao period site of **Xipo** in Henan (~4000–3000 BCE) is a fine example of how aspiring social climbers had to carefully navigate growing inequalities and the need for public cohesion. Grains – broomcorn and foxtail millet – were intensively grown and comprised the majority staple crops (Li 2013). Pigs account for ~85 percent of all animal bones excavated (Ma 2007), and, much like Dadiwan, their isotopic signals indicate that they were foddered with a regime rich in millet feed (Zhang et al. 2021). Xipo was a large site, nearly 40 ha in size, surrounded by a moat enclosing several dozen structures. Some large structures were unearthed, but graves were where social status was displayed and solidified. This was evident from the elaborate chambers adorned with diverse and labor-intensive offerings, such as ivory, jade, and painted ceramics (Li 2013). Alcoholic drinking vessels are common throughout the cemetery, but the two most richly adorned tombs were also the best equipped for elaborate alcohol consumption (Feng et al. 2021). Ritual alcohol sets were comprised of ceramic serving, mixing and drinking vessels, a stove (possibly for heating the spirits) and large vats used to process the alcohol. A combination of starch grain and fungal analysis yielded evidence for yeasts and molds connected to fermented beverages. The liquor that was produced required rare items such as rice and *Monascus* mold (which may have given the beverage a red color), but it was widely consumed – some vats found in graves could hold together more than 50 liters, enough to serve 100 people a pint each.

Summary: Neolithic Foodways in Time and Space

The agricultural revolution, as we see it today, can be perceived primarily in hindsight. For the people and communities experiencing the long transition toward dependence on cultivated crops and domesticated animals, daily meals and local cuisines were based on all available foods, wild and domesticated. Diets were quite broad in many areas, with some communities subsisting on a wide variety of wild resources even as they planted and raised cultivated plants and animals. The inhabitants of Hemudu consumed dozens of wild plants and animals right until the third millennium BCE as they grew and cultivated large amounts of domesticated rice, dogs and pigs.

These relationships would continue well into the Late Neolithic era as new foods were explored and exploited. Environmental conditions certainly shaped diets, but only to a certain degree, with communities opting to emphasize some rather than other ingredients. Food was becoming an important component of village life; the types of animals being grown, hunted and gathered greatly influenced seasonal and year-round mobility and sedentism, and further impacted the residential aspects of these sites. In various regions, including several subregions of the Yellow River Valley, agriculture was gradually assuming a central role in the subsistence economy. The landscape underwent significant transformations, with forests being cleared to make way for grain fields, with lasting ecological impacts (Lander 2021).

How food was grown and shared was directly related to sociopolitical systems. Steamers, casseroles and pots of various sizes were used to prepare different dishes, and the finely decorated wares that presented and served foods indicate just how important dining and hosting was as well. Yangshao communities lived in well-planned villages that maintained household or linage-based grain storage facilities (Figure 6). These were likely not shared freely with others, even though, for all we know, pigs and other domesticated animals were

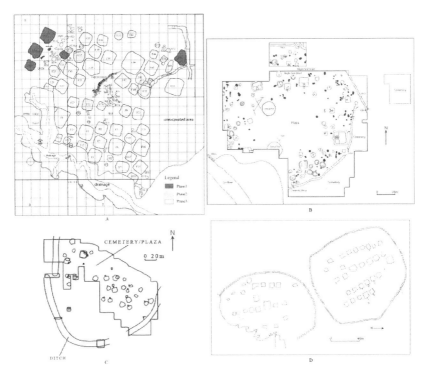

Figure 6 Layout of four Neolithic sites. A: Chahai (after Tu et al. 2022: 4); B: Jiangzhai (after Shelach 2015:74); C: Dadiwan (after Shelach 2015: 72) and D: Baiyinchanghan (after Shelach 2015: 72)

communally tended to in the central plaza. In contrast, Hongshan-period communities might have even established specialized food-production roles, where some individuals grew food to sustain full-time ritual practitioners.

Toward the Late Neolithic era, we begin to see more clearly the early formulations of social inequality. At Xipo, social hierarchy was most visibly reflected in burial treatment, where a select few were interred in large graves and accompanied by lavish offerings. The occupants of the most elaborate tombs at Xipo were missing their lower or upper incisors, a habit practiced further east (perhaps as a visual mark of group membership), and skeletal isotopic values show that the occupants of these tombs ate less millet and more rice, again differing from the rest of the community; they also suffered less from skeletal fractures and degenerative diseases (Pechenkina 2018). Could these foreigners have been elites at their village, afforded a lavish final send-off in a ceremony aimed at bringing the community together after the passing of their leaders? Or were these funerary wakes arranged by living descendants, hoping to maintain the standing their recently departed kin enjoyed? With the evidence at hand it is hard to be sure, but clearly food and drink (alcoholic beverages being suggested at a growing number of sites, e.g., Liu 2021) were an important social lubricant in the developing societies of Late Neolithic China. Competitive feasting will continue to be an important part of sociopolitical dynamics in the following centuries with the rise of large urban centers and the first cities, a topic we turn to next.

5 Interregional Interaction and Emerging Cities in the Third and Second Millennia BCE

The third and second millennia BCE were a time of growing social and political complexity in Ancient China. Enormous sites began to emerge, some with massive walls and public works that would have required millions of person hours to complete. The second half of the third millennium, when things really take off, is dominated by the settlements of the **Longshan culture** with its many local variants and types. Craft production skill increased markedly and great quantities of artifacts were produced and widely circulated throughout the ancient landscape. At the same time, new domesticates were entering from the west, chief among them sheep and goat, cattle, horses, wheat and barley, as well as technological innovations of bronze metallurgy. Famously dubbed the Longshan interaction sphere by K. C. Chang (1986), prestige goods are seen to have linked elites in a common cultural horizon through an intensified system of interregional cultural contacts, but new animals and plants would eventually impact all economic systems and culinary styles.

The rise of large urban centers and states was accompanied by new artistic styles and ideological outlooks that together are seen by many as stepping stones in the formation of Chinese civilization (see Section 6). The large centers cropping up across northern and Central China were remarkable, but how they developed and declined are still a matter of vigorous debate (see Campbell et al. 2022; Liu & Chen 2012; Shelach & Jaffe 2014; Underhill et al. 2021). Here, we will not focus on the relationship between these sites and later periods of Chinese history. Instead, we will explore how elites employed food and rituals to sustain themselves and the masses, while also gaining power during the emergence of urbanism and complex political systems. The way large centers were provisioned was a crucial component of successful urban life for both the elites and commoners residing in them, and similarly how cities went about integrating resources and people from their respective hinterlands. A steady supply of food was essential. Grain was especially important; it was good to eat and drink with. What started out as communal gatherings in the Neolithic era gave way to competitive feasting and alcohol consumption. What originally lubricated social cohesion was slowly solidifying social hierarchies as well. At the same time that these developments were taking place in the so-called traditional core of Ancient China, alternative lifeways were cropping up all across the great arc to the north, though, as we will see, their diet was not all that different, and at times no less remarkable.

Trade, Alcohol and Deepening Inequality at the Onset of the Bronze Age

Section 4 highlighted the growing importance of feasting and alcohol consumption throughout the Neolithic era in North and Central China. The Haidai region to the east, encompassing the area of the Lower Yellow River Valley to the north and the Lower Huai River Valley to the south, was no different. Beginning in the fourth millennium, this area was home to communities that mixed hunting gathering and agriculture (Jin et al. 2020). These settlements flourished into larger towns, and further development of masterful craft technologies, distinctive pottery types, and unique ceramic styles. The adoption of the fast wheel enabled craftspeople to produce a greater number of vessels quickly, leading to the creation of intricate new shapes with thinner walls (Luan 2013). Feasting was becoming a serious and significant affair. The gatherings were marked by an increasing level of sophistication, where elaborate serving dishes were expected to play a crucial role in elevating these social events.

During the Late Dawenkou culture period (~3000–2600 BCE) in this region, diet was dominated by millet, rice, dog, fish, shellfish and wild animals (mainly deer) though the variation and relative proportion of these components, especially rice, was quite large between communities (Jin et al. 2016). Only some of the variation can be explained via environmental factors (such as proximity to marine resources or rainfall amounts) as many sites inhabited the same ecological zones. Local cuisines based on food preference, not necessity, were developing (Dong et al. 2021). The site of **Yuchis**i in Anhui (~2800–2600 BCE) was surrounded by a deep moat 30 m wide enveloping an enclosed area roughly 10 ha large. Lengthy excavations here have uncovered a rich town that reflects the nature of evolving sociopolitical conditions. In it more than forty dwellings, long houses with a series of adjacent rooms, have been unearthed and around each domicile cluster was a paved plaza that included storage pits and several graves. This inner site organization has led some scholars to propose a kinship based social setup as the nuclear basis of this community where food and drink were important in the formation of group solidarity. Both cooking and serving vessel quantities found in the individual rooms would have exceeded the amount needed to support a small nuclear family, suggesting the importance of hosting larger social gatherings among the discrete kin unit. Ceramic vessels likely used for beer brewing were widely distributed throughout the site and were part of the standard domestic ceramic repertoire found at all the different clusters indicating the non-centralized organization of alcohol production. Fermented beverage remains were identified in the jars and cups from both residential and grave contexts. The fermenting vessels themselves were large and elaborately decorated, impressive centerpieces accompanying the alcohol they contained and making them visual spectacles for these larger social gatherings (Liu et al. 2022).

Status and diet were linked as well. Stable isotope analysis on skeletal remains suggests that those interred in elaborate burials may have enjoyed a better diet. At the **Dawenkou** site, several older females enjoyed meat and rice at higher rates than older males, and were buried in what are arguably the most lavish of graves (Dong et al. 2019). These same women were also honored by adorning their bodies with red pigmentation of precious cinnabar. (Notably, however, at other Dawenkou culture sites diet did not vary by gender.) Funerals were delicious (even if melancholy) events: large numbers of drinking and serving vessels were placed in graves – often numerous pitchers and containers together with dozens of goblets were placed in a single tomb. Elaborate *ge* cups, made of thin walled, finely plumed pastes, were joined by plentiful cooking and serving vessels, mostly for pork consumption, but sometimes also venison, fish and shellfish (Underhill 2002).

In the second half of the third millennium BCE, during the Longshan period, competition became fierce and those vying to better their social standing doubled their efforts (Figure 7). Households and aspiring families could display wealth, namely the accumulation of food surplus and prestigious artifacts, in a number of ways: pigs were positively correlated with richer graves, though their numbers had declined in comparison to previous periods, indicating, perhaps, restricted access to foodstuffs at this time. Large ceramic vessels were used to store, cook and serve food, and most prized were the eggshell-thin, tall-stemmed drinking cups known as *gaobingbei*. Only some burials contained these elaborate pottery vessels, indicating that their production and circulation was possibly controlled by a select number of rich families (Underhill 2002, chapter 6). Ceramic craft production reached unprecedented heights of sophistication during the Longshan period with aspiring elites competing to attract skilled laborers to produce a variety of exquisite dining wares. Increased interregional interaction during this time also brought new styles of dining and feasting, as similar vessels types were traded, produced and used in many Longshan urban sites. Liquid containers were particularly favored and elaborate sets for heating and serving beverages are found across Ancient China.

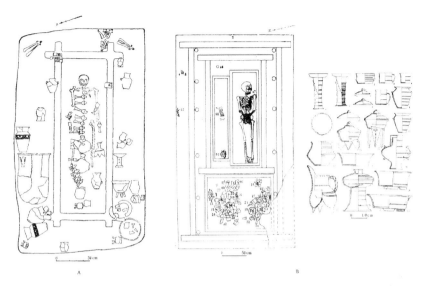

Figure 7 Grave goods and rich burials of the Dawenkou and the Longshan period (A: Dazhujiacun M17, after Shandong 1991: 171; B: Xizhufeng M1, after Shandong et al 1989: 220–223)

Previsioning Some, Manipulating Others: Tensions between City and Village

The rise of large urban sites allowed new opportunities and styles of feasting unavailable to rural communities residing in the countryside (Figure 8). The act of dining together undoubtedly played a crucial role in strengthening social bonds among a broader array of individuals, fostering new social networks that connected urban centers and small villages (Underhill 2018). The daily humdrum of making a living was no less important and feeding these large cities was a challenge in of itself. The site of **Shimao** (2300–1800 BCE) in northern Shanxi was a megacity covering more than 400 ha that would have required larger amounts of foodstuffs to sustain its population. The increased number of Longshan period sites around it (Sun et al. 2018) may have provided the backbone for its subsistence, fueled mainly by large yields of foxtail and broomcorn millet (Sheng et al. 2021). The inhabitants of Shimao focused on a limited number of domesticated animals, a mix of cattle and pig alongside newly introduced sheep and goat. While feasting may have been limited, or more commonly practiced at the so-called palatial area, as noted, these animals seem to have been enjoyed equally throughout the site with little variation between the haves and have-nots (Owlett et al. 2018). The large site of **Taosi**

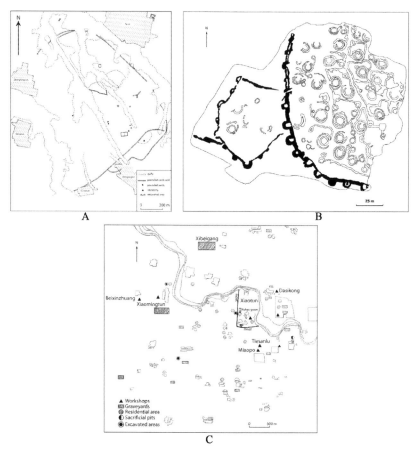

Figure 8 Layout of Longshan and Bronze Age sites. A: Taosi (after Shelach 2015: 132; B: Sanzuodian (after Shelach et al. 2011: 18; C: Yinxu (after Shelach 2015: 204)

(~2300–1900 BCE) in southern Shanxi reached a size of ~300 ha and was home to 15,000–30,000 people, according to some estimates. The site demonstrated significant social inequality, evident in the notable disparities observed in the graves as well as in the presence of a distinct elite zone within the walled city. Taosi displayed a high level of pig consumption followed by dog and only a small number of sheep/goat and cattle (Brunson et al. 2016). It is unclear how animals were raised and managed and to what extent elites enjoyed better diets or a wider selection of animals. Here too the grain of choice was millet, accompanied by some soybean (Zhao and He 2006), and while early storage facilities were situated outside the elite center, later, a new, larger storage area, possibly guarded, emerged near the central elite or palace zone, signaling a heightened emphasis on provisioning management (He 2018) – though more work is required to assess these claims (see Campbell et al. 2022). Comparing the types and quantities of animals consumed in the large cites with the smaller villages or centers outside them provides further insights into social dynamics during this time. While Taosi specialized in a select number of animal types (pig, sheep and cattle) the large site of **Zhoujiazhuang** (characterized by similar material culture) nearby exhibited little centralization and consumed more wild animals alongside these primary domesticates (Brunson et al. 2016). In contrast, both Shimao and the smaller village site of **Zhaimaoliang** ~2 ha seem to have enjoyed the same types of animals, managed them in a similar manner and were, overall, reliably self-sufficient in feeding themselves (Owlett et al. 2018).

Further to the east, in Shandong, large incipient urban centers were numerous during the Longshan period. Sites reach incredible sizes of several hundred hectares and across different parts of southern Shandong, a clear process of nucleation into large, often walled settlements can be seen (Underhill et al. 2008). As cities grew, a steady stream of grains, millet and increasingly rice was needed, though the actual role urban centers played in their organization and distribution is less clear (Crawford et al. 2005). The site of **Liangchengzhen** was an important center in southeastern Shandong. Thousands of people resided here and the city is believed to have exerted centripetal power over its surroundings. During its earlier phases, residential quarters were constructed following a common plan of several round houses facing a single courtyard with a well-worked smoothed surface. Houses were made of brick, with a single hearth in them – probably the residence of a single household with a central locus for cooking – but communal activities, such as other food preparation tasks and, possibly, consumption would have taken place in the general courtyard. During the later phases of the site, there was a noticeable increase in privacy concerns, evident through the construction of walls in areas that were previously communal courtyards. Undoubtedly this led to a decrease in inter-household interaction. (Though waste disposal was still communal as pits [garbage and storage] were unrelated to induvial houses [Underhill et al. 2021]).

The **Liangzhu** mega site (~3300–2200 BCE) in the Yangzi River Delta in Zhejiang is a marvel of landscape engineering. Up until a decade or so the site was best known for its sumptuous graves and the superb jades they contained – a single artifact demanding hundreds of hours by specialized workers to create. More recently, work done both in and out of the city has uncovered an impressive water management project that was able to control the influx of water into the valley. Destructive monsoon rains could now be funneled into a complicated system of dykes and reservoirs, creating a network of waterways for transport, as well as precious irrigation for rice paddy fields throughout the fertile valley plain (Jin et al. 2019; Liu et al. 2017a). The Neolithic cultures that inhabited the area became dependent on domesticated animals (primarily pig), but the differences in types of animals and plants being consumed, as well as their percentage in the diet, is striking. Yuan et al. (2020) show that at the Liangzhu center pigs account for 90 percent of all animal remains, while at peripheral towns they were a minor dietary component, with hunting and fishing considerably higher. One possible explanation for these differences is that pigs may have been particularly suitable for urban surroundings, scavenging through the garbage pits and trash readily available to them in a densely packed city (Dong & Yuan 2020). Though how they were controlled and how ownership was maintained remains unclear, as is how much of a nuisance roving packs of pigs (and their excrement) were for city dwellers (see discussions in Price, 2021). Rice was quite important, but it too was consumed differently across the valley; even though large granaries for grain surplus were found, the people at Liangzhu, and particularly the elites inhabiting the center, enjoyed a wider selection of water plants, legumes and fruits (including: peach, soy, jujube, melons and more) in their diets than any other community in the valley. At Liangzhu, even foxtail millet, a humble staple in the north, may have been consumed as an exotic delicacy by a select few (Wu et al. 2022b).

Steady production of grain and pork was a chief concern among the elites and commoners at **Xinzhai** (~2100–1750 BCE) in Henan Province and its adjacent village communities. A large site, it was surrounded by a ditch and rammed earth walls encircling, at its height, an area of roughly 100 ha. The site has been subject to decades of excavation and numerous studies, offering great insight into an urban center that spans several centuries. For meat and fat, Xinzhai's inhabitants focused on raising dogs, sheep, cattle and pig – the latter two accounting for nearly 50 percent of the excavated bone assemblage. Deer was also desired and made up 20 percent of the assemblage (Dai et al. 2016), indicating the importance of hunting. Millet, soy, rice and wheat were all grown and consumed by its inhabitants (Zhong et al. 2016). At Xinzhai, little (relatively speaking) processing went into grains and legumes prior to their storage. Since dehusking grain (including winnowing, threshing and so on) is quite labor-intensive, the choice to store grain in minimally processed forms (often simply the whole plant) might indicate a small-scale operation undertaken on a single household basis that was unable to mobilize the large amount of labor needed for plant shelling during the harvest (An et al. 2022). While households at the big city might have worked independently of one another, at the smaller **Dongzhao** village, communal efforts were the norm. The more intensive labor that went into grain processing at Dongzhao would have resulted in hulled grain that could be conveniently consumed when desired. Urban centers potentially strengthened relationships in certain aspects, but they also disentangled them in other ways.

The Introduction of New Domesticates in the Third and Second Millennia BCE

As we have seen, a number of important plants and animals were domesticated in China, chiefly rice, millet, pigs and later soy, as well as a variety of other grasses, grains, fruits, nuts and tubers (Sections 2 and 3). Long-distance interaction across Eurasia, beginning in the third millennium BCE, introduced Southwest Asian domesticates to China: caprines (sheep and goat), cattle, barley (*Hordeum vulgare*) and wheat (*Triticum*). This trans-Eurasian exchange brought new technologies as well, such as domesticated horses, chariots and metallurgy, via a number of passageways into the Chinese continent, the most important of which was the Hexi Corridor – a conduit of the later historical Silk Road network in western China running from Xinjiang down in Gansu. This "proto Silk Road" provided relatively convenient passageway across the Taklamakan Desert and the harsh mountain ranges of the Qinghai and the Tibetan Plateaus. This was not a unidirectional road into China, but a complex network of interactions that allowed movement of peoples, ideas and social practices across Eurasia (Flad 2018; Kuzmina 2008; Selbitschka 2018).

The provinces of Gansu, Qinghai, Ningxia and Shaanxi are where many of these domesticates were first encountered. Domesticated cattle appear in China in Gansu perhaps as early as ~3600 BCE and are found in many regions following the third millennium BC where they bred with local cattle species (Liu & Ma 2017; Lu et al. 2017). The number of cattle bones remain low for most of the third and early second millennia, and only after 2000 BCE will they become central for diet, traction, bone tool production and, perhaps most importantly, rituals (Yuan & Flad 2005). Wild sheep were hunted in northern Shaanxi at least since the fifth millennium BCE (Dodson et al. 2014), but domesticated caprines were introduced in the later part of the third millennium BCE, the earliest found in the Hexi Corridor and goats arriving after sheep (Brunson et al. 2020; Ren et al. 2022)

The introduction of wheat and barley is also a matter of debate and evidence for their presence in the third millennium BCE indicates competing land routes, such as the mountainous steppe, and even some by sea (Long et al. 2018; Zhou et al. 2020). In the far northwestern province of Xinjiang, there is evidence for third-millennium wheat, though more convincingly during the early second millennium BCE. Barley was not as well favored and is found more sparingly throughout the region during the initial introduction phase (Li 2021). Some of the earliest wheat is actually found in Shandong, in the far east, as early as the mid-third millennium BCE – though it too initially played a marginal role, accounting for less than 10 percent of total grain found at most Longshan sites (Chen et al. 2020; Guo & Jin 2019). Barley and wheat are more widely distributed and intensively cultivated in Ancient China only after 2000 BCE (Flad 2010; Lister et al. 2018; Liu et al. 2017c).

These domesticates would go on to have a massive impact on local diets and cuisines, but were initially adopted only gradually and unequally (Boivin et al. 2012; Jaffe & Flad 2018; Liu et al. 2019b; Yang et al. 2019). Prior to the introduction of these domesticates, diet and cuisine along the Hexi Corridor were quite uniform and were based on millet as the staple grain and pigs for fat and protein. At the onset of the early third millennium BCE, communities further to the west (the area through which these domesticated initially traveled), actually chose not to adopt them, and continued to raise dogs and pigs and hunt deer, while further to the east, several communities happily added sheep, goat and cattle to their bowls (Vaiglova et al. 2021). Barley and wheat were important additions to existing agricultural regimes and may have aided in efforts to more permanently settle the Tibetan Highland as they are more resistant to high-altitude conditions (d'Alpoim Guedes et al. 2015). Other communities in Central China that initially rejected wheat adopted the grain later on (Barton & An 2014). In Shandong, the introduction of wheat was also accompanied by an increase of local rice consumption as well (Ma & Jin 2017) – possibly because wheat would have been sown and harvested at different times, providing few labor conflicts with other crop management regimes. Some scholars propose a culinary explanation for the selective adoption of barley and wheat. Unlike millet that was boiled, wheat and barley would have been ground into flour and baked – a difference that may explain why they were adopted in areas like the Hexi corridor rather than the lower Yellow River Valley where millet was the all-important crop (originally in Fuller & Rowlands 2011; see Liu & Reid 2020).

I am not sure why early adoptions would preclude boiling barley and wheat or the grinding of millet into flour. (Analyzing the way ceramic vessels were used to cook foods via use-wear alteration analysis, would provide important insight into these models, but has yet to be done here.) We should not be quick to dismiss this topic, however, as wheat flour remains an important part of the controversy surrounding a bowl of noodles from the border of Gansu and Qinghai. Often dubbed the Pompeii of China, **Lajia** (~2000 BCE) was afflicted by a number of natural disasters, including earthquakes, floods and mudslides that destroyed buildings and buried families in their homes. This catastrophe, which hit the inhabitants of room F20 mid-meal, sealed and perfectly preserved their skeletal remains as well as one overturned bowl of noodles. The noodles, long and thin, were originally said to have been made from ground millet dough that were stretched to form their long shape (Lu et al. 2005). This did not sit well with those who wanted a Western (and a later date) for the origins of noodles (namely Italian pasta). For the world's first noodles to be made of millet just seemed too strange to many. Pulled noodles, *lamian*, are a central component of local northwestern cuisine today and the unique pulling method is the traditional way to make noodles that can be fried, stewed or boiled. But they are famously made from wheat, a grain that has the important viscous, glutinous protein that enables dough to be pulled and stretched. This was precisely the argument made by teams who tried to show how nearly impossible it would have been to make noodles out of millet in this way, prompting suggestions that they were made out of wheat instead (Ge et al. 2011). The excavators conducted their own experiments to show how noodles can indeed be made from millet using different traditional techniques, namely squeezing the dough through holes out of a specialized wooden rack (Lü et al. 2014). The issue is far from resolved, but it appears that people were enjoying noodles in Northwest China, made of millet or wheat (or a combination of both), at the turn of the third millennium BCE.

Climate Change, Pastoralism and the Rise of the "Other"

The introduction of new domesticates and technologies along the proto Silk Road would eventually induce large changes in subsistence and culinary preferences across China. New grains diversify routine diets and embellish monotonous cuisines, and they can aid frontiersmen and women in the settlement of challenging environmental zones. Hardy barley and drought-resistant broomcorn millet fair better in cold and dry climates than rice or foxtail millet. Additionally, as new plant species have different planting, flowering and harvesting times they can be integrated into existing cropping systems to improve soil health and provide food throughout the agricultural cycle. The species of animal societies choose to raise and consume is a key factor not only with respect to how food tastes, but also in the food system complexities they engender. Pastoralism, the intensive rearing of ruminant livestock (namely caprines and cattle) on vegetated, open spaces for subsistence purposes, is noticeably different than raising pigs in pens and chickens in sheltered coops. Pasturing animals offers an additional food source that complements available resources, unlike, say, pigs, which consume scraps, but also grain, which could have otherwise been used to feed humans. Securing suitable lands upon which to graze animals is a constant concern for herders, especially when rival groups compete over limited resources and seasonal conditions require the movement of herds between different ecological zones and elevations. Transhumance (the practice of moving herds en masse) is common among pastoralists, but just how mobile these early populations were and how central animal raising was to their economic livelihood, as well as their social identity, varied over time and place.

The third millennium BCE is also a time of presumed transformative climatic changes, the Holocene Event 3 (aka the 4.2 ka event or ~4 k BP event) being one of the most prominent environmental changes of the mid-Holocene epoch. This event, often claimed to have been global in scale, is characterized generally as one of cooling in the upper latitudes and drying elsewhere. The co-occurrence of large-scale environmental change with the introduction of sheep and goat in the third millennium BCE has been taken by some to indicate the point in time when nomadic pastoralism emerged in parts of the Eurasian Steppe. The cultural underpinnings that separated China and its people (during the Zhou and later Han periods) from the areas outside it, running in a great arc from east to east in the north, was determined in no small part by what people ate. When the people inhabiting it are mentioned in later historical texts, food often plays an important role in their disparaging characterization as barbarians: They are those who consume more meat than grain and know little of ritual propriety, aka good dining etiquette (see Pines 2005; Sterckx 2004). Even while little research has focused on foodways, communities inhabiting these regions from the second millennium BCE onward are reconstructed as practicing an early form of nomadic pastoralism (see overviews of these discussions in Jaffe et al. 2021b; Jaffe & Hein 2021; Taché et al. 2021).

The picture of a highly mobile, nomadic, lifestyle – antithetical to sedentary agricultural ways of living central to the later Sino/Barbarian Farmer/nomad divide – is a romantic way to describe those peoples who raise large ruminant herds, but one that overlooks the importance of crop raising, seasonal sedentism and less-mobile systems of agropastoralism (Honeychurch & Makarewicz 2016). While there is evidence for the importance of mobile dairy pastoralism in the Mongolian and Eurasian steppes before this time (Jeong et al. 2018; Wilkin et al. 2020) and even for cheese production in the Xinjiang Province Area at ~1500 BCE (Xie et al. 2016; Yang et al. 2014), in the areas outside the Eurasian steppe a variable picture emerges. Setting aside the skepticism raised by several studies regarding the direct connection between these climatic events and short-term socioeconomic changes, it is evident that the ~4.2KBP event's actual magnitude and duration had varying impacts on economic and subsistence practices (Jaffe et al. 2021a; see Su & Kidder 2019; Yang et al. 2019; Yuan et al. 2020).

A rapid survey across the arc, encompassing areas running to the northeast and west of China's traditional center, reveals clear and distinct culinary variations. In the provinces of Shaanxi and Ningxia, well into the second half of the third millennium BCE, hunting continued alongside millet agriculture. Some enjoyed a broad diet of fish, mollusks, birds and small mammals, while others specialized in hunting specific animals, like the wild horses that had roamed the region for countless millennia. At **Miaoliang**, for example, situated, in the far north of Shaanxi, wild horses account for nearly three-fourths of the taxa found at the site (Festa & Monteith 2022). At the turn of the second millennium, the importance of wild animals dropped and an increase in pigs alongside new domesticates began. Domesticated pigs were well known for some time but were only marginally incorporated into existing agricultural lifeways. Wild animals were the primary meat source, but when sheep and goat arrived they were more quickly incorporated as meat and possibly milk providers. Tao Shi's (2022) survey of wild taxa found at post-third-millennium BCE sites in the region finds that even if climatic shifts took place, their effects were limited as no real change in wild species can be seen, such as those linked to colder and drier environment. Tao argues instead that herbivores would have been a compelling addition to existing economic systems as they could be grazed on local grasses and thus would not compete with humans, as pigs do, for grain and other foods. In the northeast, a semiarid zone, the transition from the third to the second millennium BCE, shows even less evidence for large-scale nomadic pastoralism in places such as Jilin, Liaoning and Inner Mongolia. During the **Lower Xiajiadian** culture period, the number of sites increases dramatically and many are found across the alluvial plains where communities continued to practice dry farming agriculture centered on pigs and millet and only the gradual incorporation of sheep, goats and cattle (Shelach-Lavi et al. 2016). In fact, a new feature of this period are fortified sites and hill forts, some reaching several hectares in size. At the site of **Sanzuodian** in central Inner Mongolia, houses were built with restricted courtyards and granaries, reflecting a situation of restricted sharing of grain resources – probably the individual family/household alone (Shelach et al. 2011).

In the northwest, pastoralism may have only been practiced during the **Qijia culture** period (~2300–1600 BCE) – somewhat later than previously thought (Brunson et al. 2020; Ma et al. 2021). An initial reliance on a mix of hunted animals and domesticated pig and millet in this region slowly shifted, over several long millennia, toward sheep/goat and some cattle raising as pigs and dogs declined (Ren et al. 2022). New stable isotope studies have suggested that at this time a decrease of C4-dominated foods (millets) to a mixed C3 (rice, barley or wheat) and C4 diet can be seen across the region (see overview in Liu & Reid 2020). This is to be expected with the introduction of new wheat and barley crops, but the levels to which they were consumed was unequal across northwestern communities (Cheung et al. 2017; Liu et al. 2014) – though how much meat was consumed remains unclear (see Jaffe & Hein 2021). Recent work in the Tao River Valley in Gansu found that communities continued to practice mixed agropastoralism and sedentary lifestyles well into the late second millennium BCE. At the **Xindian culture** (~1600– 600 BCE) site of **Huizuiwa**, for example, millet was the most important crop followed by barley and wheat, nearly a millennium after these domesticates were encountered. Sheep and goat became the primary sources of meat, whereas settling near a flowing perennial river did not necessarily imply a definitive culinary preference for hunting deer or gathering and fishing aquatic resources as evidenced by scarce skeletal remains (Jaffe et al. 2021b). At the near contemporaneous **Siwa culture** (~1300–500 BCE) site of **Zhanqi**, combined use-alteration and residue analyses suggest that meals were prepared with millet grains and ruminant dairy fats (dairy, meat or both) in the distinctive saddle-shaped mouth *ma'an* cooking pot. While some have considered this vessel reflective of inferior craftsmanship (to be "expected" of simple pastoral nomads), their unique shape, highlights the exceptional level of sophistication that allowed food to be cooked in a variety of ways (Figure 9). While the three-legged *li* tripod, common across Ancient China, would have been placed in or next to the fire for boiling and stewing, the *ma'an* cooking jar, with its constricted opening and a sturdy flat bottom, could easily handle this task, and the wide surface area created by the vessel's walls

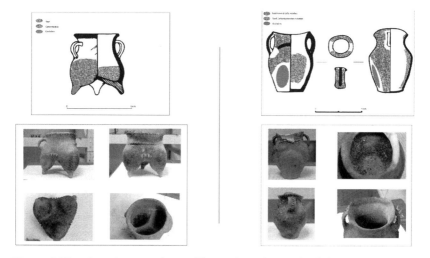

Figure 9 Use alteration remains on Siwa culture *li* vessels (left) and *ma'an* jars (right) (Images by author)

further enabled frying or sautéing when the vessel was placed on its side (Taché et al. 2021).

Summary: Foodways in Urban and Interconnected Landscapes

The third millennium BCE saw the continued importance of alcohol production and consumption – one that was slowly being co-opted by elites as yet another avenue for social climbing. What started out in the Dawenkou period as a way to ceremoniously send off beloved family members with food and drink reached enormous levels of investment over time. During the subsequent Longshan period and the latter half of the third millennium, full-time specialist were laboring away to create splendid drinking vessels that may have been used only once at funerary feast designed to impress and solidify social standings.

Many of these elites formed the central pillars of new urban centers and while they could wow subordinates with lavish parties, they may have reserved them for dignified guests or impressing competing elite factions. Current evidence suggests that some urban elites enjoyed very different meals than their lower-class neighbors did, both in and outside of the city. At Liangzhu, pigs were the favored meat source supplemented by a diverse diet of rice, water plants, legumes and fruits, while at the villages outside the center, rice dominated, alongside deer and fish. At places like Shimao, comparisons between elite and commoner residences in the city point to cuisines prepared with similar animals, grains and plants – a diet that extended to external villages as well. Ceramic containers reflected variation and growing concerns with food and cuisine as markers of status as well. Residue analysis conducted on ceramic jars, pitchers and cups from the so-called palatial area at Shimao indicate they may have held alcohol made from millet and rice and flavored with ginger or turmeric. These two spices are not native to the northern loess plateau where Shimao is located and, together with other nonlocal finds (notably musical instruments), show the degree to which foreign items were desired (He et al. 2021).

As food was becoming increasingly important for distinguishing urban dwellers from rural villagers, as well as elites from commoners, it may have also started to play a role in differentiating social groups from one other, in a limited manner. Different communities dealt with changing environments and the arrival of new domesticates (chief among them sheep, goat, wheat and barley) during the third and second millennia BCE in a number of ways, mostly by selectively incorporating these new plants and animals – though none turned to exclusive nomadic pastoralism as is sometimes suggested. The mixed agro-pastoral lifestyles that emerged are actually similar to those suggested for other

parts of prehistoric Eurasia, where flexibility and seasonal mobility characterized most forms of pastoralism. Rugged nomads, riding astride in the saddle as
they move massive ruminant herds across seas of grass, will appear much later
in history. In fact, during the late third and early second millennia BCE, sheep
and goat were readily integrated into some of the emerging urban centers. The
combination of their meat, milk, and later wool would have rendered them an
extraordinary technological package for generating and accumulating wealth.

6 From Ancient to Early China: Some Concluding Thoughts

This Element has provided an overview of foodways in Ancient China from the
arrival of the first *Homo sapiens* to the early historical periods in the first
millennium BCE. The final section is divided into two parts. The first overviews
the limited data we have on foodways in the traditional geographic core of
Ancient China and the pre-imperial dynasties that developed in it: the Xia and
Shang during the second millennium BCE, later followed by the Zhou. In the
previous sections, we met the Longshan cultures that predated these dynasties,
as well as the cultures and societies that developed alongside them, such as the
Siwa, Xiajiadian and Qijia, later in the second millennium. The sites I survey
here are some of the best known and published on and to date most scholarship
has engaged with relating the traditional dynasties to archaeological entities in
order to understand their connection to the later historical periods of the first
millennium BCE, leaving studies on foodways a frequently overlooked research
topic. Yet, even with the limited information, it is still possible to shed light on
these topics and more. Subsequently, the second part expands the concise
summaries at the end of each section. It offers a brief overview of the key
points presented and introduces new perspectives to consider while contemplat-
ing the significance of food in Ancient China.

Part I The Bronze Age: China at Last?

The Xia, Shang, and Zhou dynasties hold paramount importance in traditionally
Chinese scholarship as they are considered the foundational periods of ancient
Chinese history and culture. Pioneering archaeological work in the early twen-
tieth century confirmed the historical authenticity of the Shang dynasty, while
that of the earlier Xia remains hotly debated. In fact, only the later Shang, the
Anyang or Yinxu period (~1250–1050 BCE) is widely equated with the traditional Shang dynasty, due to the texts found at the capital that identify it as
much, leaving scholars divided on the extent to which older findings can be
attributed to earlier Shang dynastic capital centers (see overviews in Campbell
2018; Jaffe & Shelach 2014; Liu and Chen 2012). A central component of this

Figure 10 Anyang Bronzes: A. Late Shang Pou with four rams' heads; B. Late Shang Bronze Hu; C. Late Shang Bronze Gui; D. Late Shang Bronze Ya Xu Square Ding (Courtesy of Gary Todd)

debate has to do with the development of bronze vessels during the second millennium BCE that would, over the course of the next two millennia, become an indispensable apparatus of administrative ritual sacrifice and sovereign legitimacy (Figure 10). These bronze vessels were geared toward servicing the ancestors and spirts in important sacrificial ceremonies. Ancestors were summoned to join the living in fabulous rituals of food and drink to receive cult, and in return were asked to protect and lobby on behalf of their kin in the celestial realms they now inhabited. Over time, these rituals transformed into extraordinary multimedia events that encompassed music, food, dance, and the recitation of poetry (for overviews of bronzes, their use and sociopolitical importance, see, e.g., Falkenhausen 1999; Puett 2002). Some argue that ritual dinning and feasting, central to consolidation of political authority and power, were the legacy of the previous Neolithic practices we have seen (notably Chang 1983; more recently, see Li 2022). Indeed, the bronzes themselves provide one way to demarcate a common Ancient Chinese sphere external to and surrounded by peoples and cultures, such as those pastoral "Others" we met in the previous section, and whose metal artifacts (and ceramics for that matter) did in fact differ in style, ornamentation and shape.

The **Erlitou** site in Henan is a central part of this discussion, and is often taken as China's first state and the capital seat of the Xia dynasty. While this depiction is not accepted by all, the large site, roughly 300 ha, was certainly an important regional center at its prime (~1800–1550BCE). Diet was centered around millet, dog, pig, rice, soy and different fruits and nuts. Introduced through the Eurasian exchange (Section 5), cattle, as well as sheep and goats, played an increasingly important role in local cuisines – caprines were probably raised not only for their meat but also for their valuable wool (Yuan et al. 2020). Erlitou was an important center of craft goods production and might have exerted some amount of centripetal force on surrounding regions. With respect to size, level of inequality or ability to mobilize labor for public works, however, it seems on par with earlier Longshan and other late third millennium BCE sites – even bronze vessels production, while new, was limited in scale (Campbell et al. 2022; Shelach & Jaffe 2014). The development of the **Zhengzhou** site of the Erligang culture (~1600–1400 BCE), less than 100 km to the west of Erlitou, in contrast, marks a truly unprecedented political, economic and social development. The site reached almost 25 km^2 in size and would have been home to 50,000–130,000 people. Its influence expanded far beyond the city itself: archaeologists have found Erligang material culture (which some, we should point out, equate to the early Shang) as far north as Beijing and south to the Yangzi River. Provisioning such a city would have required Herculean efforts and there is some evidence to suggest an increase in the quantities of grain and legumes that were grown, in comparison to previous periods (Jia et al. 2018). Much of the site remains under the eponymous modern-day city, but what is known is that workshops of stone, bone, ceramic and even bronze were all geared toward supporting the large urban populations and providing them with tools and quotidian goods (Campbell et al. 2022).

Nearby, at the contemporary site of **Yanshi** (~200ha), zooarchaeological work has uncovered a predominance of pig followed by cattle and some sheep and goat – possibly more important for wool production; wild animals, in contrast, are hardly found (You & Wu 2021). Architectural grandeur clearly demarcated walled-off elite zones at the site, and pits containing large amounts of plants, animals and ceramic vessels provide clues to the feasts held in these locations (Reinhart 2015): while commoner areas across the site yielded high numbers of *li* tripods for cooking, *yan* vessels for steaming and an assortment of mixing and serving bowls, the elite/palace area contained high amounts of large *Weng* urns, *guan* jars, *pen* basins and other storage and serving dishes, many far larger than those found elsewhere across the site. These events many not have been open to the public, as there is some evidence to suggest that smaller-scale feasts were taking place among simpler residential areas, either emulating palace life or simply sharing a fine communal meal among equals.

As impressive as Erlitou and Zhengzhou were, nothing like Shang **Anyang** (~1250–1050 BCE) in Henan, nor the kingdom its rulers controlled, existed before it. This was a huge city, home to possibly hundreds of thousands of people, that was the center of a network of political alliances and subordinates and encompassed natural resources and agricultural lands. The urban landscape was a patchwork of administrative centers, ritual performative zones, a palace complex, large-scale workshops of bone and metal, residences for commoners and elites and a large mortuary district, which, in total, spanned some 30 km² (Campbell et al. 2022). Commoners and elites alike certainly needed to be fed, but at Anyang so too did the dead ancestors, spirts and gods. In fact, feeding the living and the dead may have been entangled in more than one way. Grain, mostly millet and animals, such as cattle, sheep, pig, dog, and even humans were all offered, and quantities could be quite substantial (Campbell 2018). A century of archaeological work at Anyang is complemented by textual evidence, in the form of ritual oracle bone inscriptions, much of it concerned with agriculture, food and sacrificial offerings. One inscription reads:

> On Dinghai the King should offer one hundred (jars?) of millet beer, one hundred sheep, one hundred cattle. *H32044+H32686* (Campbell 2023, p. 98)

The spirits and ancestors consumed these sacrifices, which were believed to have been a significant source of sustenance for the masses as well, who enjoyed a portion of the offerings. Even in non-elite contexts beef surpassed all other animals, including pork, as a source of meat suggesting widescale participations in these rituals or some form of meat distribution system following their sacrifice. Indeed, decades of zooarchaeological work has uncovered the staggering numbers of animals consumed at the site, possibly half a million head of cattle and hundreds of thousands of pigs and an equal amount of sheep and goat (Campbell 2018). The great settlement Shang may have lacked the massive outer walls of Erligang Zhengzhou, or public works found in earlier Longshan centers, but it was unparalleled when it came to incredible and frequent feasts (Yuan & Flad 2005), which aided in solidifying and reinforcing existing social hierarchies (Campbell et al. 2022).

External animal provisions, pig, caprines and cattle, had to be brought in from the surrounding villages and countryside. Tribute is often discussed in Shang oracle bone inscriptions with particular emphasis on cattle as being "levied," "taken" and "received" from afar. Pigs may have been supplied from nearby hinterlands where grain was grown as well (Li 2011). Campbell (2023) notes that at least 70 percent of food consumed at Anyang would have to have been brought in from well beyond the settlement limits and hinterlands. A particular concern with successful and bountiful harvests is common in oracle bone inscriptions (charmingly, this is also where we are told that excrement, human and animal waste, was applied to fields). Grain may have been more closely managed, grown on crownlands and levied from nearby lords and commoners and stored in large royal granaries (Campbell 2018).

Recent work in the rural village of Guandimiao indicates that animals, cattles and pigs, were likely sent to the great settlement Shang. Based on animal age at death survivorship curve comparisons between Xiaomintun (a residential neighborhood at Anyang) and Gaundimiao, it is clear that pigs and cows were raised with optimal meat production parameters in mind at Anyang, while at Guandimiao, in contrast, other considerations were at play as a wide range of ages can be seen in the mortality profile. Male adult pigs are notably absent from the bone assemblage, while female pigs lived to older ages than expected (Hou et al. 2019). Thus, it is fair to suggest that males were sent off to Anyang while females were kept alive to continue pumping out piglets, though they were also slaughtered to provide for an occasional meal. In fact, unlike their Anyang counterparts, Guandimiao villagers ate little meat – not even wild animals that would have been available to them were found (Li et al. 2018b).

At Anyang, wild animals were restricted to elites, who enjoyed wild buffalo, boar and elaphur deer. The hunting of wild animals, primary large mammals, was becoming a central part of elite life and identity. The skill and the specialized equipment it demanded (Shang lords hunted with chariots, hounds and nets), the unpredictable outcomes and, always, the dangers it entailed made hunting an exclusionary practice. Interestingly, wild animals were consumed by elites, but were rarely sacrificed; only domesticated animals, the products of human civilization (including humans), were regularly offered to and consumed by the spirits – to date, thousands of human sacrifices have been found at Anyang and recent isotopic work suggests that most were foreigners brought in and kept alive for several years and fed a simple millet diet until they were killed (Cheung et al. 2017). At the same time, the ritual vessels in which domesticated pigs, sheep, cows and humans were offered were adorned with wild beasts and fantastical zoomorphic images. The wild and domestic spheres were intertwined and hierarchies of who, what and how they were acquired and consumed was a constant concern in the Shang world: ancestors and spirts ate both domesticated humans and animals via sacrifice, elites ate wild beasts they themselves hunted as well as domesticated animals they commissioned, while the common folk had to make do with domesticated animals, their meat often acquired only through large ritual offerings overseen by lords and high nobles of the state (Jaffe & Campbell 2021).

These eating hierarchies are directly related to the ceremonial aspect of Shang life, specifically those of the elites. The lives and daily meals of peasants and common folk at Anyang remain largely unknown to us. How often, for example, they would have enjoyed meat remains unclear even if they were privy to portions of ritual sacrifices. What is clear is that when meat was consumed, what could be eaten was a defining aspect of social status in Shang society.

The Western Zhou Period (~1050–770BCE): A Cooking Pot Like No Other

At the turn of the first millennium BCE, a new power reigned over China. The Zhou dynasty that succeeded the Shang (having defeated them in military conflict) did so claiming the mandate of heaven was on their side. Feasting, excessive alcohol consumption and moral debauchery were often seen by later historians as a central contributing factor for the Shang downfall, their loss of power and legitimacy to the Zhou. Archaeology has shown that the practice of performing ritual sacrifices in bronze vessels was in fact carried on from the Shang, but decades of analysis have found an overall decline in drinking vessels and the increasing emphasis on containers of meat and grain. Clearly the Zhou did change the ritual to some extent, as they chose to moderate the consumption of intoxicating substances.

Once we reach the first millennium BCE, historical texts provide better and more reliable accounts of this period. Many of the ritual bonze vessels themselves were inscribed and a number of important well-known texts are thought to have been composed during this time. These provide some contemporary evidence with which to reconstruct ancient lifeways, at least for the elites and upper echelons of society. Yet a number of contributing factors have created a situation where more is known about foodways, cuisine and diet during the pre-Zhou periods. The reason for this is partly due to the abundance of historical information available from the Zhou period, which makes archaeological data less prominent in importance, especially in its latter half. However, the primary reason is likely related to the grand questions surrounding the nature of the Zhou polity, their rise and fall, and their connections to Imperial China, which are of significant importance. For those interested in reconstructing the nature of the Zhou dynasty and polity that shared its name, why study broken ceramic sherds, animal bones and burnt seeds of the simple commoners when we can consult texts and inspect elaborate bronze vessels, the artifacts of powerful elites? Indeed, how could the study of simple pottery vessels found in small, seemingly

Figure 11 A Bronze Age *li* cooking vessel from Shandong

unimportant, rural villages provide insight into the nature of complicated empires and the affairs of the state?

As we have seen throughout this Element, archaeologically inspired studies on foodways have much to add to these discussions. Elsewhere, my colleagues and I (Jaffe et al. 2018) suggested that by focusing on food and foodways we gain a powerful tool with which to rethink the very nature of the Zhou polity: as the Zhou state is believed to have spread across much of China from its center in the Wei River Valley Plain, the finding of Zhou-style bronze ritual vessels, but also ceramics used to cook and serve food, is often taken as good evidence for the arrival of Zhou power (and possibly people) to a given locale and, as such, are often used to demarcate the extent of the growing Zhou polity. Investigating use-alteration marks found on pottery vessels across frontier zones of contact between the Zhou and indigenous people reveals a more complex story (Jaffe et al. 2018). Even as most Zhou-style ceramics found at different communities look the same, they were not used in the same ways. At these villages, simple diets relied heavily on millet and were supplemented, to some extent, with animal fat and protein but more likely with vegetables and leafy greens. While these ingredients were prepared using similar Zhou-style *li* tripods, across the ancient landscape local communities used these same cooking vessels in different ways: Some made soups and stews that required boiling large amounts of water and stock whereas others utilized them for dishes that required very little liquid at all. Several communities only minimally incorporated Zhou-style ceramics into their kitchens or dinner tables, preferring to maintain their culinary traditions in smaller gatherings, while others were quick to enlarge the new Zhou-style pots to be shared in large communal meals (Jaffe et al. 2018).

I think these variable practices highlight the many different ways Zhou-style pottery was being used across the landscape; the findings of Zhou-style ceramics alone cannot be used to demarcate the boundaries of a Zhou state or the arrival of Zhou people. Zhou power was potent and pervasive to be sure, but it was not absolute or overwhelming. People were still able to choose what to do with their Zhou-style pot – specifically, how to incorporate them into existing practices or create new cuisines. Think about it this way: future archaeologists would be wrong to think that Sweden physically colonized the world just because IKEA pots are found in countless homes across the planet. Garbage dumps will indeed provide them with good information on the plants and animals consumed to showcase differences in dietary staples among different regions where similar IKEA kitchenware is found, but if archeologists inspected the pots' chemical residue contents and examined the way they were used to cook food in them, they would quickly discover a wealth of ingredients and cooking techniques as diverse as the culinary traditions produced daily in kitchens around the world. Perhaps then the Zhou landscape (and even the polity that shared its name) was not as unified and homogeneous either. Culinary variation, at least, seems to suggest as much.

Foodways are central to reconstructing the development of cultures and societies, their political institutions and lifeways – not just their diet. They give voice to the silent masses seldom talked about in historical treatises and their remains are rarely, if ever, visually impressive enough to be showcased in museum galleries. But even a broken pot sherd can question and refine grand stories about powerful empires. If given the chance, the humble cooking pot can help us retell the history of Ancient China.

Part II Cuisine and Identity: An Ever-Evolving Relationship

Summarizing the main takeaways or conclusions for an Element like this is not a straightforward task. Even so, certain observations can be made, along with key points and considerations that should be remembered when exploring the topic of food in Ancient China. A number of clear developments can be seen, such as the ability to extract more calories and food stuffs from the natural environment via improvement of tools and technologies. Humans were experts at exploiting their environments; They developed specialized tools to hunt animals, collect nuts, grains, fruits and tubers and process them in ways that made them safe to consume and also delicious to eat. Making the most of one's environment did not mean the menu was fixed or dull. The invention of pounding and grinding tools and the creation of ceramic cooking vessels were impressive achievements, though they appear to have not been crucial to the survival of ancient human groups, as much as they enabled people to enhance flavors and broaden meal items. Indeed, even before they began to cultivate plants and animals, culinary preferences were forming, spurring some human groups to craft specialized tools useful for obtaining some foods, while they neglected others that were widely available and easily acquirable.

The gradual shift toward sedentism and agricultural lifeways was not a straightforward unilineal evolutionary process – even if it appears this way to us in hindsight. Across the ancient landscape, communities who practiced settled lifeways differed with respect to residential investment and annual occupation intensity. Unlike other parts of the world where early Neolithization is accompanied by the collective seasonal assembly of hunter-gatherer groups, there is little evidence for similar developments until the later parts of the Neolithic era. Feasting and food sharing were important team-building exercises in Ancient China, where alcohol and meat, mainly pork, would have acted as a compelling social adhesive. At the same time, increased sedentism and reliance on agriculture turned out to be a mixed bag. The Middle Neolithic era was one of good times but also of deteriorating personal and communal health. The growing reliance on millets and rice is one likely explanation for rising levels of teeth wear and dental caries in adults, as well as iron deficiency and anemia – especially in children. Isotopically, members of different communities differ only little with respect to diet, as did their internal gender differentiations, indicating equal access to foods, but dental stress is found more widely among women (Pechenkina 2018). Tooth-wear declined in the subsequent Longshan and Bronze Age periods, perhaps a result of careful sifting practices that eliminated hard stones and pebbles. Boiling foods for longer would have produced dishes that were also easier on teeth. Other markers of health changes related to diet worsened over time, including the wider prevalence of anemia among adult populations and even marked decrease in physical stature (Pechenkina et al. 2002).

Were declining health, diets focused on several staples and growing agricultural dependence simply the price of urbanism and technological advances? In the Late Neolithic era, wealth inequality reached levels we would recognize in our societies today; elites were now separated from the commoners not only in the material wealth they were able to amass for their final rites, but also in life as well. Over time, the upper classes did enjoy higher levels of meat in their diets and could afford to finance trade of exotic foodstuffs. Throughout most of the Neolithic era, social disparities existed, but communities embraced cohabitating residential arrangements. Over the third millennium, elites began residing in larger domiciles that were further physically separated from the masses in secluded habitats. The influx of new domesticates entering China at this time – sheep, goat, horse, possibly cattle, wheat and barley – were gradually incorporated into existing lifeways and varied in the extent to which they supported incipient urbanism, deepening social inequalities and the formation of new forms of social identity as well.

Food was a key factor in all of these social and political developments. First, the increase in social complexity was fueled, in part, by agricultural intensification needed to feed the growing populations as well as support the upper classes by generating their the basic wealth. Often, foodstuffs provided the foundation upon which the structure of a deepening unequal society was established. What you ate was an important marker of status, and exotic foods, the variety in daily diet and the amount of meat one had access to all accentuated social divisions. These differences played into other emerging identities, such as the dichotomy between village and city and later the "us and them" characterizing distinct sociopolitical systems. Inequalities of various form differed in severity from place to place, but at the end of the second millennium, some of the largest and most sophisticated polities the ancient world has ever known emerged in Ancient China.

Readers should note that the overviews here have been far from exhaustive and some topics could not be covered in depth, particularly those pertaining to the sophistication of these incredible polities. For example, salt was a primary concern for early political enterprises in China and the Shang dynasty has even been credited with expanding into Shandong, the far east, in an effort to control the lucrative salt resources available around the Bohai sea (see Liu & Chen 2012). It is hard to discuss control over these resources, but clearly there were specialized salt-producing sites in the area around this time that continued into the first millennium BCE (Wei 2016). Work done on the Zhongba site, roughly 200 km downriver along the Yangzi from Chongqing City, provides insights into these early endeavors: Early occupation at ~2000 BCE yielded specialized equipment for salt production and its storage, involving boiling brine to reduce liquid and crystalize the salt for consumption along with clay lined pits to avoid seepage (Flad et al. 2005). Large vats may have been used to store brine or even to ferment large fish sauces or other preserved products. The number of fish bones increased markedly overtime, as did the importance of fishing nets (alongside a decline in hooks), during a time when salt production increased as well – though the real "boom" will take place only during the latter first millennium BCE (Flad 2005).

It is also important to keep in mind that although we have overviewed the history of Ancient China as one of a series of changes and developments in political, technological and economic realms, readers should not perceive this as a unilineal social evolution. Even as one can hardly compare the size and complexity of, say, Shang Anyang (30 km²) with prehistoric Jiangzhai (~2ha), over the course of the Neolithic and Longshan periods, the many communities and people who inhabited the ancient landscape experienced ebbs and flows of centralization, autonomy and dependency. These cultures and people should not be seen to have been slaves to the inevitable progress of history, but as those who actively participated in and shaped their own unfolding pasts. In fact, some third-millennium communities in the east, in Shandong, Anhui and Jiangsu Provinces, may have even abandoned large-scale pig farming and returned to hunting elk and deer as their main meat resources (Yi et al. 2021a). This recent study requires further corroboration, but if widespread, could even change the way Many view farming: agriculture may not have been the one-way path some would have us believe.

Additionally, it is often quite difficult, in hindsight, to uncover primary catalysts for change. Were the shifts from pork to venison a sensible reaction to changing climatic conditions? Or were they simply a matter of shifting tastes? Disparate communities factored in external inputs and changing circumstances differently. Similarly, we should not be tempted to attribute first appearances of cuisines, dishes or ingredients as their point of inception and subsequent incorporation into the larger repertoire of Chinese cuisine. The finding of 4,000-year-old noodles, whatever they were made of, on the border of the Qinghai and Gansu Provinces, does not mean that noodles were a mainstay item of culinary traditions moving forward in time. Regional variation was very much the norm from the earliest of times and almost all foods experienced periods of popularity, decline and resurgence. During the late second millennium, sites of the Guanzhong Basin, Sika deer were hunted extensively. In this context, meat may not have been the primary target; rather, the focus could have been on the antlers, with older males being hunted instead of the younger, tastier juveniles (Li et al. 2021). At the same time, absence of physical evidence does not necessarily mean noodles, found again only during the Han, were avoided for thousands of years. Absence of evidence is not evidence of absence, especially when we remember how rarely organic foodstuffs are preserved in the material record.

I began this Element by contending that we should avoid projecting recent historical knowns on to the distant past, even when we can use them as a starting point and guide to investigate Ancient China's culinary developments. Nevertheless, even with thousands of years separating them, the deep past and the present are connected. The flavors and cooking traditions of regional cuisines are linked through familiar ingredients and tastes that did not disappear or change entirely. How closely they resemble the past and through which strands they are related I leave for the readers to decide for themselves.

Bibliography

Allaby, R., Stevens, C., Kistler, L. & Fuller, D. (2022). Emerging evidence of plant domestication as a landscape-level process. *Trends in Ecology and Evolution*, **37**(3), 268–279.

An, J., Kirleis, W., Zhao, C. & Jin, G. (2022). Understanding crop processing and its social meaning in the Xinzhai period (1850–1750 cal BCE): A case study on the Xinzhai site, China. *Vegetation History and Archaeobotany*, **31**(3), 261–277.

An, J. & Wang, Y. (1972). Mi Xian Dahuting Han dai huaxiang shimu he bihua mu (Han dynasty stone relief and mural tombs at Dahuting Village in Mi County). *Wenwu*, **1972**(10), 49–62.

Anderson, E. N. (1988). *The food of China*. New Haven, CT: Yale University Press.

Barton, L. & An, C. (2014). An evaluation of competing hypotheses for the early adoption of wheat in East Asia. *World Archaeology*, **46**(5), 775–798.

Barton, L., Bingham, B., Sankaranarayanan, K. et al. (2020). The earliest farmers of Northwest China exploited grain-fed pheasants not chickens. *Scientific Reports*, **10**(1), 2556. https://doi.org/10.1038/s41598-020-59316-5

Barton, L., Newsome, S. D., Chen, F. H. et al. (2009). Agricultural origins and the isotopic identity of domestication in northern China. *Proceedings of the National Academy of Sciences*, **106**(14), 5523–5528.

Bar-Yosef, O. (2002). The Upper Paleolithic revolution. *Annual Review of Anthropology*, **31**, 363–393.

Bar-Yosef, O., Eren, M. I., Yuan, J., Cohen, D. J. & Li, Y. (2012). Were bamboo tools made in prehistoric Southeast Asia? An experimental view from South China. *Quaternary International*, **269**, 9–21.

Bestel, S., Bao, Y., Zhong, H., Chen, X. & Liu, L. (2018). Wild plant use and multi-cropping at the Early Neolithic Zhuzhai site in the Middle Yellow River region, China. *The Holocene*, **28**(2), 195–207.

Boaretto, E., Wu, X., Yuan, J. et al. (2009). Radiocarbon dating of charcoal and bone collagen associated with early pottery at Yuchanyan Cave, Hunan Province, China. *Proceedings of the National Academy of Sciences*, **106**(24), 9595–9600.

Bogaard, A., Allaby, R., Arbuckle, N. et al. (2021). Reconsidering domestication from a process archaeology perspective. *World Archaeology*, **53**(1), 56–77.

Boivin, N., Fuller, D. Q. & Crowther, A. (2012). Old World globalization and the Columbian exchange: Comparison and contrast. *World Archaeology*, **44** (3), 452–469.

Bray, T. (ed.) (2003). *The archaeology and politics of food and feasting in early states and empires*. New York: Plenum.

Brunson, K., He, N. & Dai, X. (2016). Sheep, cattle, and specialization: New zooarchaeological perspectives on the Taosi Longshan. *International Journal of Osteoarchaeology*, **26**(3), 460–475.

Brunson, K., Lele, R., Xin, Z. et al. (2020). Zooarchaeology, ancient mtDNA, and radiocarbon dating provide new evidence for the emergence of domestic cattle and caprines in the Tao River Valley of Gansu Province, Northwest China. *Journal of Archaeological Science: Reports*, **31**, 102262.

Cai, D., Zhang, N., Zhu, S. et al. (2018). Ancient DNA reveals evidence of abundant aurochs (*Bos primigenius*) in Neolithic Northeast China. *Journal of Archaeological Science*, **98**, 72–80.

Campbell, R. (2018). *Violence, kinship and the early Chinese state: The Shang and their world*. Cambridge: Cambridge University Press.

Campbell, R. (2023). Feeding the great settlement: Preliminary notes on the Shang animal economy. In L. Atici & B. Arbuckle (eds.), *Food provisioning in complex societies*. Boulder: University Press of Colorado, pp. 92–107.

Campbell, R., Jaffe, Y., Kim, C., Sturm, C. & Jaang, L. (2022). Chinese Bronze Age political economies: A complex polity provisioning approach. *Journal of Archaeological Research*, **30**(1), 69–116.

CASS (Chinese Academy of Social Sciences) (2001). *Mengcheng Yuchisi- Wanbei xinshiqi shidai juluo yicun de fajue yu yanjiu (Mengcheng Yuchisi· Excavation and research of the Neolithic settlement in Wanbei)*. Beijing: Kexue Press.

CASS, IA (Chinese Academy of Social Sciences) (2010). *Zhongguo kaoguxue: Xinshiqi shidaijuan (Chinese archaeology: Neolithic)*. Beijing: Kexue Press.

Chang, K. C. (ed.) (1977). *Food in Chinese culture: Anthropological and historical perspectives*. New Haven, CT: Yale University Press.

Chang, K. C. (1983). *Art, myth, and ritual: The path to political authority in Ancient China*. Cambridge, MA: Harvard University Press.

Chang, K. C. (1986). *The archaeology of Ancient China*. New Haven, CT: Yale University Press.

Chen, N., Cai, Y., Chen, Q. et al. (2018). Whole-genome resequencing reveals world-wide ancestry and adaptive introgression events of domesticated cattle in East Asia. *Nature Communications*, **9**(1), 2337. https://doi.org/10.1038/s41467-018-04737-0

Chen, X., Yu, S.-Y., Wang, Q. et al. (2020). More direct evidence for early dispersal of bread wheat to the eastern Chinese coast ca. 2460–2210 BC. *Archaeological and Anthropological Sciences*, **12**(10), 233. https://doi.org/10.1038/s41467-018-04737-0

Cheung, C., Jing, Z., Tang, J. & Richards, M. P. (2017). Social dynamics in early Bronze Age China: A multi-isotope approach. *Journal of Archaeological Science: Reports*, **16**, 90–101.

Cohen, D. J., Bar-Yosef, O., Wu, X., Patania, I. & Goldberg, P. (2017). The emergence of pottery in China: Recent dating of two early pottery cave sites in South China. *Quaternary International*, **441**, 36–48.

Craig, O. E., Saul, H., Lucquin, A. et al. (2013). Earliest evidence for the use of pottery. *Nature*, **496**(7445), 351–354.

Crawford, G. (2017). Plant domestication in East Asia. In J. Habu, P. V. Lape & J. W. Olsen (eds.), *Handbook of East and Southeast Asian archaeology*. New York: Springer, pp. 421–435.

Crawford, G., Underhill, A., Zhao, Z. et al. (2005). Late Neolithic plant remains from northern China: Preliminary results from Liangchengzhen, Shandong. *Current Anthropology*, **46**(2), 309–317.

Cucchi, T., Hulme-Beaman, A., Yuan, J. & Dobney, K. (2011). Early Neolithic pig domestication at Jiahu, Henan Province, China: Clues from molar shape analyses using geometric morphometric approaches. *Journal of Archaeological Science*, **38**(1), 11–22.

Dai, L. L., Li, Z. P., Zhao, C. Q. et al. (2016). An isotopic perspective on animal husbandry at the Xinzhai site during the initial stage of the legendary Xia dynasty (2070–1600 BC). *International Journal of Osteoarchaeology*, **26**(5), 885–896.

Dal Martello, R. (2022). The origins of multi-cropping agriculture in southwestern China: Archaeobotanical insights from third to first millennium B.C. Yunnan. *Asian Archaeology*, **6**(1), 65–85.

d'Alpoim Guedes, J. (2011). Millets, rice, social complexity, and the spread of agriculture to the Chengdu Plain and Southwest China. *Rice*, **4**(3), 104–113.

d'Alpoim Guedes, J., Lu, H., Hein, A. M. & Schmidt, A. H. (2015). Early evidence for the use of wheat and barley as staple crops on the margins of the Tibetan Plateau. *Proceedings of the National Academy of Sciences*, **112**(18), 5625–5630.

d'Alpoim Guedes, J., Lu, H., Li, Y. et al. (2014). Moving agriculture onto the Tibetan Plateau: The archaeobotanical evidence. *Archaeological and Anthropological Sciences*, **6**(3), 255–269.

Dennell, R., Martinón-Torres, M., Bermúdez de Castro, J.-M. & Xing, G. (2020). A demographic history of late Pleistocene China. *Quaternary International*, **559**, 4–13.

d'Errico, F., Pitarch Martí, A., Wei, Y. et al. (2021). Zhoukoudian Upper Cave personal ornaments and ochre: Rediscovery and reevaluation. *Journal of Human Evolution*, **161**, 103088.

Dietler, M. & Hayden, B. (eds.) (2001). *Feasts: Archaeological and ethnographic perspectives on food, politics, and power*. Washington, DC: Smithsonian Institution Press.

Dodson, J., Dodson, E., Banati, R. et al. (2014). Oldest directly dated remains of sheep in China. *Scientific Reports*, **4**(1), 7170.

Dong, N. & Yuan, J. (2020). Rethinking pig domestication in China: Regional trajectories in Central China and the Lower Yangtze Valley. *Antiquity*, **94** (376), 864–879.

Dong, Y., Chen, S., Ambrose, S. H. et al. (2021). Social and environmental factors influencing dietary choices among Dawenkou culture sites, Late Neolithic China. *The Holocene*, **31**(2), 271–284.

Dong, Y., Lin, L., Zhu, X., Luan, F. & Underhill, A. P. (2019). Mortuary ritual and social identities during the late Dawenkou period in China. *Antiquity*, **93** (368), 378–392.

Drennan, R. D., Lu, X., & Peterson, C. E. (2017). A place of pilgrimage? Niuheliang and its role in Hongshan society. *Antiquity*, **91**(355), 43–56.

Eda, M., Itahashi, Y., Kikuchi, H. et al. (2022). Multiple lines of evidence of early goose domestication in a 7,000-y-old rice cultivation village in the lower Yangtze River, China. *Proceedings of the National Academy of Sciences*, **119**(12), e2117064119.

Eda, M., Lu, P., Kikuchi, H. et al. (2016). Reevaluation of early Holocene chicken domestication in northern China. *Journal of Archaeological Science*, **67**, 25–31.

Elston, R. G. & Brantingham, P. J. (2002). Microlithic technology in northern Asia: A risk-minimizing strategy of the Late Paleolithic and Early Holocene. *Archaeological Papers of the American Anthropological Association*, **12**(1), 103–116.

Elston, R. G., Guanghui, D. & Dongju, Z. (2011). Late Pleistocene intensification technologies in northern China. *Quaternary International*, **242**(2), 401–415.

Elvin, M. (2004). *The retreat of the elephants: An environmental history of China*. New Haven, CT: Yale University Press.

Falkenhausen, L. (1999). Late Western Zhou taste. *E'tudes Chinoises* 18: 134–178.

Feng, S., Liu, L., Wang, J. et al. (2021). Red beer consumption and elite utensils: The emergence of competitive feasting in the Yangshao culture, North China. *Journal of Anthropological Archaeology*, **64**, 101365.

Festa, M. & Monteith, F. (2022). Between plain and plateau: Micro-transitions in zooarchaeological landscapes in the Guanzhong region of Northwest China. *Land*, **11**(8), 1269. https://doi.org/10.3390/land11081269

Flad, R. (2018). Where did the Silk Road come from? In J. Rudolph & M. Szonyi (eds.), *The China Questions: Critical insights into a rising power*. Cambridge, MA: Harvard University Press, pp. 237–243.

Flad, R. (2010). Early wheat in China: Results from new studies at Donghuishan in the Hexi Corridor. *The Holocene*, **20**(6), 955–965.

Flad, R. (2005). Evaluating fish and meat salting at prehistoric Zhongba, China. *Journal of Field Archaeology*, **30**(3), 231–253.

Flad, R., Zhu, J., Wang, C. et al. (2005). Archaeological and chemical evidence for early salt production in China. *Proceedings of the National Academy of Sciences*, **102**(35), 12618–12622.

Frantz, L. A. F., Mullin, V. E., Pionnier-Capitan, M. et al. (2016). Genomic and archaeological evidence suggest a dual origin of domestic dogs. *Science*, **352** (6290), 1228–1231.

Fullagar, R., Hayes, E., Chen, X., Ma, X., & Liu, L. (2021). A functional study of denticulate sickles and knives, ground stone tools from the Early Neolithic Peiligang culture, China. *Archaeological Research in Asia*, **26**, 100265.

Fuller, D. Q., Qin, L., Zheng, Y. et al. (2009). The domestication process and domestication rate in rice: Spikelet bases from the Lower Yangtze. *Science*, **323**(5921), 1607–1610.

Fuller, D. Q. & Rowlands, M. (2011). Ingestion and food technologies: Maintaining differences over the long-term in West, South and East Asia. In T. J. Wilkinson, S. Sherratt & J. W. Bennett (eds.), *Interweaving worlds: Systematic interactions in Eurasia, 7th to 1st millennia BC*. Oxford: Oxbow Books, pp. 36–60.

Fuller, D. Q. & Stevens, C. J. (2019). Between domestication and civilization: The role of agriculture and arboriculture in the emergence of the first urban societies. *Vegetation History and Archaeobotany*, **28**(3), 263–282.

Gao, X., Guan, Y., Chen, F. et al. (2014). The discovery of Late Paleolithic boiling stones at SDG 12, north China. *Quaternary International*, **347**, 91–96.

Gao, Y. (2021) *Zhongguo Dongbei diqu gongyuanqian sanqiannianqian de wenhua yanjin yu shehuui fazhan (Cultural evolution and social development in Northeast China before 3000 BC)*. Doctoral Diss. Jilin University.

Ge, W., Liu, L., Chen, X., & Jin, Z. (2011). Can noodles be made from millet? An experimental investigation of noodle manufacture together with starch grain analyses. *Archaeometry*, **53**(1), 194–204.

Ge, W., Liu, L., Huang, W. et al. (2021). Neolithic bone meal with acorn: Analyses on crusts in pottery bowls from 7000 BP Hemudu, China. *International Journal of Osteoarchaeology*, **31**(6), 1138–1154.

Goldin, P. R. (ed.). (2018). *Routledge handbook of Early Chinese history*. New York: Routledge.

Graeber, D. & Wengrow, D. (2021). *The dawn of everything: A new history of humanity*. New York: Farrar, Straus and Giroux.

Guo, R. & Jin, G. (2019). Xianqin shiqi haidai diqu de maizuo nongye (Study on the wheat agriculture in the pre-Qin period of Haidai Region), *Disiji Yanjiu*, **39**(1), 144–160.

Hastorf, C. A. (2016). *The social archaeology of food: Thinking about eating from prehistory to the present*. Cambridge: Cambridge University Press.

Hastorf, C. A. & Foxhall, L. (2017). The social and political aspects of food surplus. *World Archaeology*, **49**(1), 26–39.

Hayden, B. (2009). The proof is in the pudding: Feasting and the origins of domestication. *Current Anthropology*, **50**(5), 597–601.

He, N. (2018). Taosi: An archaeological example of urbanization as a political center in prehistoric China. *Archaeological Research in Asia*, **14**, 20–32.

He, Y., Liu, L., Sun, Z., Shao, J. & Di, N. (2021). "Proposing a toast" from the first urban center in the north Loess Plateau, China: Alcoholic beverages at Shimao. *Journal of Anthropological Archaeology*, **64**, 101352.

Hebei Sheng Wenwu Yanjiusuo et al. (2010). 1997 nian Hebei Xushui Nanzhuangtou yizhi fajue baogao (Report on the 1997 Excavations at the Nanzhuangtou Site, Xushui County, Hebei Province, *Kaogu Xuabao* **2010** (3), 361–392.

Henan First Team, CASS et al. (2020), Henan Xinzheng Peiligang yizhi 2018–2019 fajue (The excavation of the Peiligang site of Xinzheng city, Henan, 2018–2019) *Kaogu Xuebao* **2020** (4), 521–546.

Höllmann, T. (2014). *The land of the five flavors: A cultural history of Chinese cuisine*. New York: Columbia University Press.

Honeychurch, W. & Makarewicz, C. A. (2016). The archaeology of pastoral nomadism. *Annual Review of Anthropology*, **45**(1), 341–359.

Hou, Y., Campbell, R., Zhang, Y. & Li, S. (2019). Animal use in a Shang village: The Guandimiao zooarchaeological assemblage. *International Journal of Osteoarchaeology*, **29**(2), 335–345.

Hou, L., Li, J., Deng, H. & Guo, Y. (2021). Hubei Xushui Nanzhuangtou yizhi dongwu goge de wending tongweisu fenxi (Stable isotope analysis of animal skeletons at Nanzhuangtou Site, Xushui, Hebei Province). *Kaogu*, **2021** (5), 107–114.

Hu, Y., Shang, H., Tong, H. et al. (2009). Stable isotope dietary analysis of the Tianyuan 1 early modern human. *Proceedings of the National Academy of Sciences*, **106**(27), 10971–10974.

Hua, Z., Xinwei, L., Weilin, W., Liping, Y. & Zhijun, Z. (2020). Preliminary research of the farming production pattern in the Central Plain area during the Miaodigou Period. *Quaternary Sciences*, **40**(2), 472–485.

Huan, X., Lu, H., Jiang, L. et al. (2021). Spatial and temporal pattern of rice domestication during the early Holocene in the lower Yangtze region, China. *The Holocene*, **31**(9), 1366–1375.

Hunt, H. V., Shang, X. & Jones, M. K. (2018). Buckwheat: A crop from outside the major Chinese domestication centres? A review of the archaeobotanical, palynological and genetic evidence. *Vegetation History and Archaeobotany*, **27**(3), 493–506.

Jaffe, Y. & Campbell, R. (2021). To eat or not to eat? Animals and categorical fluidity in Shang society. *Asian Perspectives*, **60**(1), 157–177.

Jaffe, Y., Castellano, L., Shelach-Lavi, G. & Campbell, R. B. (2021a). Mismatches of scale in the application of paleoclimatic research to Chinese archaeology. *Quaternary Research*, **99**, 14–33.

Jaffe, Y. & Flad, R. K. (2018). Prehistoric globalizing processes in the Tao River Valley, Gansu, China? In N. Boivin & M. Frachetti (eds.), *Globalization in prehistory: Contact, exchange, and the "people without history,"* pp. 131–161. Cambridge: Cambridge University Press.

Jaffe, Y. & Hein, A. (2021). Considering change with archaeological data: Reevaluating local variation in the role of the ~4.2 k BP event in Northwest China. *The Holocene*, **31**(2), 169–182.

Jaffe, Y., Hein, A., Womack, A. et al. (2021b). Complex pathways towards emergent pastoral settlements: New research on the Bronze Age Xindian culture of Northwest China. *Journal of World Prehistory*, **34**(4), 595–647.

Jaffe, Y., Wei, Q. & Zhao, Y. (2018). Foodways and the archaeology of colonial contact: Rethinking the Western Zhou expansion in Shandong. *American Anthropologist*, **120**(1), 55–71.

Jeong, C., Wilkin, S., Amgalantugs, T. et al. (2018). Bronze Age population dynamics and the rise of dairy pastoralism on the eastern Eurasian steppe. *Proceedings of the National Academy of Sciences*, **115**(48), E11248–E11255.

Jia, S., Zhang, J., Yang, Y. et al. (2018). Zhengzhou Shangcheng yizhi tanhua zhiwu yicun fuxuan jieguo yu fenxi (A preliminary study of the charred plant remains from the Zhengzhou Shangcheng site). *Jianghan Kaogu*, **2018**(2), 97–114.

Jiang, L. (2013). The Kuahuqiao site and culture. In A. Underhill (ed.), *A companion to Chinese archaeology*. Malden, MA: Wiley, pp. 535–554.

Jin, G., Chen, S., Li, H. et al. (2020). The Beixin Culture: Archaeobotanical evidence for a population dispersal of Neolithic hunter-gatherer-cultivators in northern China. *Antiquity*, **94**(378), 1426–1443.

Jin, G., Wagner, M., Tarasov, P. E., Wang, F. & Liu, Y. (2016). Archaeobotanical records of Middle and Late Neolithic agriculture from Shandong Province, East China, and a major change in regional subsistence during the Dawenkou Culture. *The Holocene*, **26**(10), 1605–1615.

Jin, G., Wu, W., Zhang, K., Wang, Z., & Wu, X. (2014). 8000-Year old rice remains from the north edge of the Shandong highlands, East China. *Journal of Archaeological Science*, **51**, 34–42.

Jin, Y., Mo, D., Li, Y. et al. (2019). Ecology and hydrology of early rice farming: Geoarchaeological and palaeo-ecological evidence from the Late Holocene paddy field site at Maoshan, the Lower Yangtze. *Archaeological and Anthropological Sciences*, **11**(5), 1851–1863.

Jordan, P. & Zvelebil, M. (eds.). (2009). *Ceramics before farming: The dispersal of pottery among prehistoric Eurasian hunter-gatherers*. London: Routledge.

Kuzmina, E. (2008). *The prehistory of the Silk Road*. Philadelphia: University of Pennsylvania Press.

Lander, B. (2021). *The king's harvest: A political ecology of China from the first farmers to the first empire*. New Haven, CT: Yale University Press.

Lander, B., Schneider, M. & Brunson, K. (2020). A history of pigs in China: From curious omnivores to industrial pork. *Journal of Asian Studies*, **79**(4), 865–889.

Larson, G., Karlsson, E. K., Perri, A. et al. (2012). Rethinking dog domestication by integrating genetics, archeology, and biogeography. *Proceedings of the National Academy of Sciences*, **109**(23), 8878–8883.

Larson, G., Liu, R., Zhao, X. et al. (2010). Patterns of East Asian pig domestication, migration, and turnover revealed by modern and ancient DNA. *Proceedings of the National Academy of Sciences*, **107**(17), 7686–7691.

Lee, G., Crawford, G. W., Liu, L. & Chen, X. (2007). Plants and people from the Early Neolithic to Shang periods in North China. *Proceedings of the National Academy of Sciences*, **104**(3), 1087–1092.

Lee, G., Crawford, G. W., Liu, L., Sasaki, Y. & Chen, X. (2011). Archaeological soybean (Glycine max) in East Asia: Does size matter? *PLOS ONE*, **6**(11), e26720.

Lee, Y. (2007). Centripetal settlement and segmentary social formation of the Banpo tradition. *Journal of Anthropological Archaeology*, **26**(4), 630–675.

Li, F., Kuhn, S. L., Chen, F. et al. (2018a). The easternmost Middle Paleolithic (Mousterian) from Jinsitai Cave, North China. *Journal of Human Evolution*, **114**, 76–84.

Li, M. (2022). Libation ritual and the performance of kingship in early China. *Journal of Anthropological Archaeology*, **65**, 101370.

Li, S., Campbell, R. B. & Hou, Y. (2018b). Guandimiao: A Shang village site and its significance. *Antiquity*, **92**(366), 1511–1529.

Li, W., Tsoraki, C., Lan, W. et al. (2019a). Cereal processing technique inferred from use-wear analysis at the Neolithic site of Jiahu, Central China. *Journal of Archaeological Science: Reports*, **23**, 939–945.

Li, X. (2013). The later Neolithic period in the Central Yellow River Valley area, c.4000–3000 BC. In A. Underhill (ed.), *A companion to Chinese archaeology*. Malden, MA: Wiley, pp. 213–235.

Li, X., Song, X., Xiaomin, W. et al. (2019b). Preliminary study on the living environment of hominin occupation at Fuyan cave, Daoxian County, Hunan. *Quaternary Sciences*, **39**(6), 1476–1486.

Li, Y. (2021). Agriculture and palaeoeconomy in prehistoric Xinjiang, China (3000–200 BC). *Vegetation History and Archaeobotany*, **30**(2), 287–303.

Li, Y., Zhang, C., Chen, H., Wang, Z. & Qian, Y. (2021). Sika deer in Bronze Age Guanzhong: Sustainable wildlife exploitation in ancient China? *Antiquity*, **95**(382), 940–954.

Li, Z. (2011). Yinxu Xiaomintun yizhi chutu jiazhu de siwang nianling yu xiangguan wenti yanjiu (A study on death age of domestic pig excavated from Xiaomintun site of Yin dynasty and related research), *Jianghan Kaogu* **2011**(4), 89–96.

Li, Z., Wu, X.-J., Zhou, L. et al. (2017). Late Pleistocene archaic human crania from Xuchang, China. *Science*, **355**(6328), 969–972.

Lister, D., Jones, H., Oliveira, H. et al. (2018). Barley heads east: Genetic analyses reveal routes of spread through diverse Eurasian landscapes. *PLOS ONE*, **13**(7), e0196652.

Liu, B., Wang, N., Chen, M. et al. (2017a). Earliest hydraulic enterprise in China, 5,100 years ago. *Proceedings of the National Academy of Sciences*, **114**(52), 13637.

Liu, L. (2021). Communal drinking rituals and social formations in the Yellow River Valley of Neolithic China. *Journal of Anthropological Archaeology*, **63**, 101310.

Liu, L. & Chen, X. (2012). *The archaeology of China: From the Late Paleolithic to the early Bronze Age*. Cambridge: Cambridge University Press.

Liu, L., Ge, W., Bestel, S. et al. (2011). Plant exploitation of the last foragers at Shizitan in the Middle Yellow River Valley China: Evidence from grinding stones. *Journal of Archaeological Science*, **38**(12), 3524–3532.

Liu, L. & Ma, X. (2017). The zooarchaeology of Neolithic China. In U. Albarella, M. Rizzetto, H. Russ, K. Vickers & S. Viner-Daniels (eds.), *The Oxford handbook of zooarchaeology*. Oxford: Oxford University Press, pp. 304–318.

Liu, L., Wang, J., Chen, R., Chen, X. & Liang, Z. (2022). The quest for red rice beer: Transregional interactions and development of competitive feasting in Neolithic China. *Archaeological and Anthropological Sciences*, **14**(4), 78. https://doi.org/10.1007/s12520-022-01545-y

Liu, L., Wang, J., Levin, M. et al. (2019a). The origins of specialized pottery and diverse alcohol fermentation techniques in Early Neolithic China. *Proceedings of the National Academy of Sciences*, **116**(26), 12767–12774.

Liu, T., Liu, Y., Sun, Q. et al. (2017b). Early Holocene groundwater table fluctuations in relation to rice domestication in the middle Yangtze River basin, China. *Quaternary Science Reviews*, **155**, 79–85.

Liu, W., Martinón-Torres, M., Cai, Y. et al. (2015). The earliest unequivocally modern humans in southern China. *Nature*, **526**(7575), 696–699.

Liu, X., Jones, P., Motuzaite, G. et al. (2019b). From ecological opportunism to multi-cropping: Mapping food globalisation in prehistory. *Quaternary Science Reviews*, **206**, 21–28.

Liu, X., Lightfoot, E., O'Connell, T. et al. (2014). From necessity to choice: Dietary revolutions in west China in the second millennium BC. *World Archaeology*, **46**(5), 661–680.

Liu, X., Lister, D., Zhao, Z. et al. (2017c). Journey to the east: Diverse routes and variable flowering times for wheat and barley en route to prehistoric China. *PLOS ONE*, **12**(11), e0187405.

Liu, X. & Reid, R. (2020). The prehistoric roots of Chinese cuisines: Mapping staple food systems of China, 6000 BC–220 AD. *PLOS ONE*, **15**(11), e0240930.

Long, T., Leipe, C., Jin, G. et al. (2018). The early history of wheat in China from 14 C dating and Bayesian chronological modelling. *Nature Plants*, **4**(5), 272–279.

Lu, H., Li, Y., Zhang, J. et al. (2014). Component and simulation of the 4,000-year-old noodles excavated from the archaeological site of Lajia in Qinghai, China. *Chinese Science Bulletin*, **59**(35), 5136–5152.

Lu, H., Yang, X., Ye, M. et al. (2005). Culinary archaeology: Millet noodles in Late Neolithic China. *Nature*, **437**(7061), 967–968.

Lu, P., Brunson, K., Yuan, Ji. & Li, Z. (2017). Zooarchaeological and genetic evidence for the origins of domestic cattle in Ancient China. *Asian Perspectives*, **56**(1), 92–120.

Lu, R. (2022). Houli wenhua de fenqi niandai yu difang leixing (The periodization, dating and regional type of the Houli culture). *Dongnan Wenhua* **2022** (1), 91–103.

Lü, T. (2010). Early pottery in South China. *Asian Perspectives*, **49**(1), 1–42.

Luan, F. (2013). The Dawenkou culture in the lower Yellow River and Huai River basin areas. In A. Underhill (ed.), *A companion to Chinese archaeology*. Malden, MA: Wiley, pp. 411–434.

Luo, Y. (2012). *Zhongguo guda zhu lei xunhua siyang yu yishi xing [The domestication, feeding and ritual uses of pigs in ancient China]*. Beijing: Kexue Press.

Ma, M., Ren, L., Li, Z. et al. (2021). Early emergence and development of pastoralism in Gan-Qing region from the perspective of isotopes. *Archaeological and Anthropological Sciences*, **13**(6), 93. https://doi.org/10.1007/s12520-021-01331-2

Ma, X. (2005). *Emergent social complexity in the Yangshao culture: Analyses of settlement patterns and faunal remains from Lingbao, western Henan, China (c. 4900–3000 BC)*, Oxford: Archaeopress.

Ma, Y. & Jin, G. (2017). Haidai Longshan wenhua nongzuowu leixing ji quyu tedian fenxi (Crop assemblages and regional characteristics of Longshan culture in Haidai region). In F. Luan, F. Wang & Y. Dong (eds.). *Longshan wenhua yu zaoqi wenming*. Beijing: Wenhua Press, pp. 161–178

Matuzevičiūtė, G., & Liu, X. (2021). Prehistoric agriculture in China: Food globalization in prehistory. https://doi.org/10.1093/acrefore/9780199389414.013.168

Mcbrearty, S. & Brooks, A. S. (2000). The revolution that wasn't: A new interpretation of the origin of modern human behavior. *Journal of Human Evolution*, **39**(5), 453–563.

McGovern, P., Zhang, J., Tang, J. et al. (2004). Fermented beverages of pre- and proto-historic China. *Proceedings of the National Academy of Sciences*, **101** (51), 17593–17598.

Nakajima, T., Hudson, M. J., Uchiyama, J., Makibayashi, K. & Zhang, J. (2019). Common carp aquaculture in Neolithic China dates back 8,000 years. *Nature Ecology & Evolution*, **3**(10), 1415–1418.

Owlett, T., Hu, S., Sun, Z. & Shao, J. (2018). Food between the country and the city: The politics of food production at Shimao and Zhaimaoliang in the Ordos Region, northern China. *Archaeological Research in Asia*, **14**, 46–60.

Pan, Y. & Yuan J. (2018). Xinshiqi shidai zhi xian Qin shiqi changjiang xiaoyou de shengye xingtai yanjiu (Study on the subsistence of the lower Yangtze River region from Neolithic to Pre-Qin period). *Nanfang Wenwu*, **2018**(4), 111–125.

Pan, Y., Zheng, Y. & Chen, C. (2017). Human ecology of the Early Neolithic Kuahuqiao culture in East Asia. In J. Habu, P. V. Lape & J. W. Olsen (eds.), *Handbook of East and Southeast Asian archaeology*, New York: Springer, pp. 347–377.

Patania, I., Goldberg, P., Cohen, D. et al. (2019). Micromorphological and FTIR analysis of the Upper Paleolithic early pottery site of Yuchanyan cave, Hunan, South China, *Geoarchaeology*, **35**(2), 143–163.

Patania, I. & Jaffe, Y. (2021). Collaboration, not competition: A geoarchaeological approach to the social context of the earliest pottery. *Journal of Anthropological Archaeology*, **62**, 101297.

Pechenkina, E. A., Benfer, R. A. & Zhijun, W. (2002). Diet and health changes at the end of the Chinese Neolithic: The Yangshao/Longshan transition in Shaanxi Province. *American Journal of Physical Anthropology*, **117**(1), 15–36.

Pechenkina, K. (2018). Of millets and wheat: Diet and health on the central plain of China during the Neolithic and Bronze Age. In P. Goldin (ed.), *Routledge handbook of early Chinese history*. New York: Routledge, pp. 39–60.

Peng, F., Wang, H. & Gao, X. (2014). Blade production of Shuidonggou Locality 1 (Northwest China): A technological perspective. *Quaternary International*, **347**, 12–20.

Peterson, C. & Shelach, G. (2012). Jiangzhai: Social and economic organization of a Middle Neolithic Chinese village. *Journal of Anthropological Archaeology*, **31**(3), 265–301.

Pines, Y. (2005). Beasts or humans: Pre-imperial origins of Sino-Barbarian dichotomy. In R. Amitai & M. Biran (eds.), *Mongols, Turks, and Others: Eurasian nomads and the sedentary world*. Leiden: Brill, pp. 59–102.

Prendergast, M. E., Yuan, J. & Bar-Yosef, O. (2009). Resource intensification in the Late Upper Paleolithic: A view from southern China. *Journal of Archaeological Science*, **36**(4), 1027–1037.

Price, M. (2021). *Evolution of a taboo: Pigs and people in the ancient Near East*. New York: Oxford University Press.

Price, M. & Hongo, H. (2019). The archaeology of pig domestication in Eurasia. *Journal of Archaeological Research*, **28**, 557–615.

Price, T. & Bar-Yosef, O. (2011). The origins of agriculture: New data, new ideas. An introduction to supplement 4. *Current Anthropology*, **52**(S4), S163–S174.

Puett, M. 2002. *To become a god: Cosmology, sacrifice, and self-divinization in early China*. Cambridge, MA: Harvard University Press.

Qu, T., Bar-Yosef, O., Wang, Y. & Wu, X. (2013). The Chinese Upper Paleolithic: Geography, chronology, and techno-typology. *Journal of Archaeological Research*, **21**(1), 1–73.

Ran, W. (2022). *Sustaining ritual: Provisioning a Hongshan pilgrimage center at Niuheliang*, PhD thesis, University of Pittsburgh, Pittsburgh, PA.

Reed, K. (2021). Food systems in archaeology: Examining production and consumption in the past. *Archaeological Dialogues*, **28**(1), 51–75.

Reinhart, K. (2015). Ritual feasting and empowerment at Yanshi Shangcheng. *Journal of Anthropological Archaeology*, **39**, 76–109.

Ren, L., Yang, Y., Qiu, M. et al. (2022). Direct dating of the earliest domesticated cattle and caprines in northwestern China reveals the history of pastoralism in the Gansu-Qinghai region. *Journal of Archaeological Science*, **144**, 105627.

Selbitschka, A. (2018). The early Silk Road(s). In D. Ludden (ed.), *Oxford research encyclopedia of Asian history*. New York: Oxford University Press. https://oxfordre.com/asianhistory/view/10.1093/acrefore/9780190277727.001.0001/acrefore-9780190277727-e-2

Shandong Institute of Archaeology and Cultural Relics (1991). Juxian Dazhujiacun Dawenkou wenhua muzang (Tombs of the Dawenkou culture at Dazhujia village, Juxian county). *Kaogu Xuebao*, **1991**(2), 167–206.

Shandong Institute of Archaeology and Cultural Relics and Linqu County Cultural Relics Preservation Office (1989). Linquxian Xizhufeng Longshan wenhua chongguomu de qingli (Excavation of the Longshan Cultural burial with double outer coffins at Xizhufeng, Linqu County). *Haidai Kaogu*, **1989**, 219–224.

Shandong Institute of Archaeology and Cultural Relics and Chengziya Museum (2012). Zhangqiushi Xihe Yizhi 2008 nian kaogu fajue baogao (Excavation report of the Xihe site in 2008, Zhangqiu). *Haidai Kaogu* **2012**, 67–138.

Shang, H., Tong, H., Zhang, S., Chen, F. & Trinkaus, E. (2007). An early modern human from Tianyuan Cave, Zhoukoudian, China. *Proceedings of the National Academy of Sciences*, **104**(16), 6573–6578.

Shelach, G. (2006). Economic adaptation, community structure, and sharing strategies of households at early sedentary communities in northeast China. *Journal of Anthropological Archaeology*, **25**(3), 318–345.

Shelach, G. (2015). *The archaeology of early China from prehistory to the Han dynasty.* Cambridge: Cambridge University Press.

Shelach, G. & Jaffe, Y. (2014). The earliest states in China: A long-term trajectory approach. *Journal of Archaeological Research*, **22**(4), 327–364.

Shelach, G., Raphael, K. & Jaffe, Y. (2011). Sanzuodian: The structure, function and social significance of the earliest stone fortified sites in China. *Antiquity*, **85**(327), 11–26.

Shelach-Lavi, G., Teng, M., Goldsmith, Y. et al. (2019). Sedentism and plant cultivation in northeast China emerged during affluent conditions. *PLOS ONE*, **14**(7), e0218751.

Shelach-Lavi, G., Teng, M., Goldsmith, Y. et al. (2016). Human adaptation and socioeconomic change in northeast China: Results of the Fuxin Regional Survey. *Journal of Field Archaeology*, **41**(4), 467–485.

Shelach-Lavi, G. & Tu, D. (2017). Food, pots and socio-economic transformation: The beginning and intensification of pottery production in North China. *Archaeological Research in Asia*, **12**, 1–10.

Shen, H. & Li, X. (2021). From extensive collection to intensive cultivation, the role of fruits and nuts in subsistence economy on Chinese Loess Plateau. *Archaeological and Anthropological Sciences*, **13**(4), 61.

Sheng, P., Hu, Y., Sun, Z. et al. (2020). Early commensal interaction between humans and hares in Neolithic northern China. *Antiquity*, **94**(377), 1395–1395.

Sheng, P., Shang, X., Zhou, X. et al. (2021). Feeding Shimao: Archaeobotanical and isotopic investigation into early urbanism (4200–3000 BP) on the northern Loess Plateau, China. *Environmental Archaeology*. DOI: 10.1080/14614103.2021.2009995

Shi, T. (2022). Understanding the transition to agropastoralism in North China: Archaeobotanical and zooarchaeological evidence. *Archaeological Research in Asia*, **29**, 100345.

Shoda, S., Lucquin, A., Sou, C. I. et al. (2018). Molecular and isotopic evidence for the processing of starchy plants in Early Neolithic pottery from China. *Scientific Reports*, **8**(1), 17044.

Smith, M. L. (2015). Feasts and their failures. *Journal of Archaeological Method and Theory*, **22**(4), 1215–1237.

Song, G. (2013). Recent research on the Hemudu culture and the Tianluoshan site. In A. Underhill (ed.), *A companion to Chinese archaeology*. Malden, MA: Wiley, pp. 555–573.

Song, J., Wang, L. & Fuller, D. Q. (2019a). A regional case in the development of agriculture and crop processing in northern China from the Neolithic to Bronze Age: Archaeobotanical evidence from the Sushui River survey,

Shanxi Province. *Archaeological and Anthropological Sciences*, **11**(2), 667–682.

Song, Y., Cohen, D. J., Shi, J. et al. (2017). Environmental reconstruction and dating of Shizitan 29, Shanxi Province: An early microblade site in north China. *Journal of Archaeological Science*, **79**, 19–35.

Song, Y., Grimaldi, S., Santaniello, F. et al. (2019b). Re-thinking the evolution of microblade technology in East Asia: Techno-functional understanding of the lithic assemblage from Shizitan 29 (Shanxi, China). *PLOS ONE*, **14**(2), e0212643.

Song, Y., Sun, B., Gao, Y. & Yi, H. (2019c). The environment and subsistence in the lower reaches of the Yellow River around 10,000 BP: Faunal evidence from the bianbiandong cave site in Shandong Province, China. *Quaternary International*, **521**, 35–43.

Song, Y., Wang, J., Liu, Y. & Wang, Z. (2021). Xihe yizhi 2008 nian chutu dongwu yicun fenxi-jianlun Houli wenhua shiqi de yulei xiaofei (Animal remains unearthed in the 2008 excavation at the Xihe site: With a discussion on fish consumption in the Houli Cultural Period). *Jianghan Kaogu*, **2021**(1), 112–119.

Spengler, R. (2020). Anthropogenic seed dispersal: Rethinking the origins of plant domestication. *Trends in Plant Science*, **25**(4), 340–348.

Sterckx, R. (2004). Food and philosohy in early China. In R. Sterckx (ed.), *Of tripod and palate: Food, politics and religion in traditional China*. New York: Palgrave Macmillan, pp. 34–61.

Stevens, C. J. & Fuller, D. Q. (2017). The spread of agriculture in eastern Asia: Archaeological bases for hypothetical farmer/language dispersals. *Language Dynamics and Change*, **7**(2), 152–186.

Stevens, C. J., Shelach-Lavi, G., Zhang, H., Teng, M. & Fuller, D. Q. (2021). A model for the domestication of *Panicum miliaceum* (common, proso or broomcorn millet) in China. *Vegetation History and Archaeobotany*, **30**(1), 21–33.

Su, K. & Kidder, T. (2019). Humans and climate change in the middle and lower Yellow River of China. *Quaternary International*, **521**, 111–117.

Sun, B., Wagner, M., Zhao, Z. et al. (2014). Archaeological discovery and research at Bianbiandong Early Neolithic cave site, Shandong, China. *Quaternary International*, **348**, 169–182.

Sun, H. & Jiang, L. (2016). Zhejiang Pujiang Shangshan yizhi Shangshan wenhua taoqi leixingxue yanjiu jixiangguan wenti (Typological research and related issues of the Shangshan cultural pottery from the Shangshan site, Pujiang, Zhejiang). *Nanfang Wenwu* **2016**(3), 89–108.

Sun, X., Wen, S., Lu, C. et al. (2021). Ancient DNA and multimethod dating confirm the late arrival of anatomically modern humans in southern China. *Proceedings of the National Academy of Sciences*, **118**(8), e2019158118.

Sun, Z., Shao, J., Liu, L. et al. (2018). The first Neolithic urban center on China's north Loess Plateau: The rise and fall of Shimao. *Archaeological Research in Asia*, **14**, 33–45.

Taché, K., Jaffe, Y., Craig, O. et al. (2021). What do "barbarians" eat? Integrating ceramic use-wear and residue analysis in the study of food and society at the margins of Bronze Age China. *PLOS ONE*, **16**(4), e0250819.

Tong, H. (2008). Quaternary hystrix (rodentia, mammalia) from North China: Taxonomy, stratigraphy and zoogeography, with discussions on the distribution of hystrix in Palearctic Eurasia. *Quaternary International*, **179**(1), 126–134.

Tu, D., Shelach-Lavi, G. & Fung, Y. (2022). Economy, sharing strategies and community structure in the Early Neolithic village of Chahai, Northeast China. *Journal of Anthropological Archaeology*, **67**, 101420.

Twiss, K. (2019). *The archaeology of food: Identity, politics, and ideology in the prehistoric and historic past*. Cambridge: Cambridge University Press.

Underhill, A. (2002). *Craft production and social change in Northern China*, New York: Kluwer Academic/Plenum.

Underhill, A. (ed.). (2013). *A companion to Chinese archaeology*. Malden, MA: Wiley-Blackwell.

Underhill, A. (2018). Urbanization and new social contexts for consumption of food and drink in northern China. *Archaeological Research in Asia*, **14**, 7–19.

Underhill, A., Cunnar, G., Luan, F. et al. (2021). Urbanization in the eastern seaboard (Haidai) area of northern China: Perspectives from the Late Neolithic site of Liangchengzhen. *Journal of Anthropological Archaeology*, **62**, 101288.

Underhill, A., Feinman, Gary. M. et al. (2008). Changes in regional settlement patterns and the development of complex societies in southeastern Shandong, China. *Journal of Anthropological Archaeology*, **27**(1), 1–29.

Vaiglova, P., Reid, R. E. B., Lightfoot, E. et al. (2021). Localized management of non-indigenous animal domesticates in northwestern China during the Bronze Age. *Scientific Reports*, **11**(1), 15764.

Wang, C., Lu, H., Gu, W. et al. (2019). The development of Yangshao agriculture and its interaction with social dynamics in the Middle Yellow River region, China. *The Holocene*, **29**(1), 173–180.

Wang, J. & Jiang, L. (2022). Intensive acorn processing in the early Holocene of southern China. *The Holocene*, **32**(11), 1305–1316.

Wang, J., Jiang, L. & Sun, H. (2021). Early evidence for beer drinking in a 9000-year-old platform mound in southern China. *PLOS ONE*, **16**(8), e0255833.

Wang, L. & Qu, X. (2018) Pengtoushan wenhua fenqi yu leixing (The classification and periodization of Pengtoushan culture), *Jianghan Kaogu* **2018** (3), 68-80.

Wang, L. & Sebillaud, P. (2019). The emergence of early pottery in East Asia: New discoveries and perspectives. *Journal of World Prehistory*, **32**(1), 73–110.

Wang, Y., Zhang, S., Gu, W. et al. (2015). Lijiagou and the earliest pottery in Henan Province, China. *Antiquity*, **89**(344), 273–291.

Wei, Q. (2016). Ceramic management at salt production sites during the early Bronze Age in northern Shandong, China. *Asian Archaeology* **4**, 33–46.

Wei, X., Li, Y., Wen, T. et al. (2022). Zhongguo kaogu de guoji hua fenxi-cong Zhongwai kaogu qikan lunwen shuju chufa (Analyses of Internationalisation of Chinese archaeology: Based on the data of papers published in Chinese and foreign archaeological journals). *Cultural Relics in Southern China*, **2022**(1), 30–40

Weisskopf, A., Deng, Z., Qin, L. & Fuller, D. Q. (2015). The interplay of millets and rice in Neolithic Central China: Integrating phytoliths into the archaeobotany of Baligang. *Archaeological Research in Asia*, **4**, 36–45.

Wilkin, S., Ventresca Miller, A., Taylor, W. T. et al. (2020). Dairy pastoralism sustained eastern Eurasian steppe populations for 5,000 years. *Nature Ecology & Evolution*, **4**(3), 346–355.

Wu, W. (2019). Haidai diqu Houli wenhua shengye jingji de yanjiu yu sikao (The study and reflection on the subsistence economy of the Houli culture in the Haidai area). *Kaogu*, **2019**(8), 103–115.

Wu, X., Zhang, C., Goldberg, P. et al. (2012). Early pottery at 20,000 years ago in Xianrendong cave, China. *Science*, **336**(6089), 1696–1700.

Wu, Y., Tao, D., Wu, X., Liu, W. & Cai, Y. (2022a). Diet of the earliest modern humans in East Asia. *Frontiers in Plant Science*, **13**. https://doi.org/10.3389/fpls.2022.989308

Wu, Y., Wang, C., Zhang, Z. & Ge, Y. (2022b). Subsistence, environment, and society in the Taihu lake area during the Neolithic era from a dietary perspective. *Land*, **11**(8), 1229.

Xiang, H., Gao, J., Yu, B. et al. (2014). Early Holocene chicken domestication in northern China. *Proceedings of the National Academy of Sciences*, **111** (49), 17564–17569.

Xie, L. (2018). Scapulae for shovels: Does raw material choice reflect techno-logical ease and low cost in production? *Journal of Archaeological Science*, **97**, 77–89.

Xie, L., Lu, X., Sun, G. & Huang, W. (2017). Functionality and morphology: Identifying *si* agricultural tools among Hemudu scapular implements in eastern China. *Journal of Archaeological Method and Theory*, **24**(2), 377–423.

Xie, M., Shevchenko, A., Wang, B. et al. (2016). Identification of a dairy product in the grass woven basket from Gumugou Cemetery (3800 BP, northwestern China). *Quaternary International*, **426**, 158–165.

Xu, Z. & Chen, S. (2019). Shangshan wenhua juzhi liudongxing fenxi: Zaoqi nongye xingtai yanjiu (Analysis on the liquidity of Shangshan cultural residence: Study on early agricultural forms). *Nanfang Wenwu* **2019** (4): 165–173.

Yang, J., Zhang, D., Yang, X. et al. (2022). Sustainable intensification of millet–pig agriculture in Neolithic North China. *Nature Sustainability*, **5**(9), 780–786.

Yang, S., Deng, C., Zhu, R. & Petraglia, M. (2020). The Paleolithic in the Nihewan Basin, China: Evolutionary history of an early to late Pleistocene record in eastern Asia. *Evolutionary Anthropology: Issues, News, and Reviews*, **29**(3), 125–142.

Yang, X., Chen, Q., Ma, Y. et al. (2018a). New radiocarbon and archaeobota-nical evidence reveal the timing and route of southward dispersal of rice farming in South China. *Science Bulletin*, **63**(22), 1495–1501.

Yang, X., Wan, Z., Perry, L. et al. (2012). Early millet use in northern China. *Proceedings of the National Academy of Sciences*, **109**(10), 3726–3730.

Yang, X., Wu, W., Perry, L. et al. (2018b). Critical role of climate change in plant selection and millet domestication in North China. *Scientific Reports*, **8** (1), 7855.

Yang, Y., Ren, L., Dong, G. et al. (2019). Economic change in the prehistoric Hexi Corridor (4800–2200 bp), North-West China. *Archaeometry*, **61**(4), 957–976.

Yang, Y., Shevchenko, A., Knaust, A. et al. (2014). Proteomics evidence for kefir dairy in early Bronze Age China. *Journal of Archaeological Science*, **45**, 178–186.

Yi, H., Ga, H. & Xu, J. (2021a). Jiangsu dongtai Kaizhuang yizhi dongwu yicun yanjiu baogao (A study of faunal remains from the Kaizhuang site in Dongtai, Jiangsu Province). *Nanfang Wenwu* **2021**(3), 80–91.

Yi, M., Gao, X., Chen, F., Pei, S. & Wang, H. (2021b). Combining sedentism and mobility in the Palaeolithic–Neolithic transition of northern China: The site of Shuidonggou locality 12. *Antiquity*, **95**(380), 292–309.

You, Y. & Wu, Q. (2021). The uses of domesticated animals at the early bronze age city of wangjinglou, China. *International Journal of Osteoarchaeology*, **31**(5), 789–800.

Yuan, J. (1999). Lun Zhongguo Xinshiqi shidai jumin huoqu roushi ziyuan de fangshi (On the ways people in Neolithic settlements in China obtained meat resources). *Kaogu Xuebao* **1999**(1), 1–22.

Yuan, J., Campbell, R., Castellano, L. & Xianglong, C. (2020). Subsistence and persistence: Agriculture in the central plains of China through the Neolithic to Bronze Age transition. *Antiquity*, **94**(376), 900–915.

Yuan, J. & Dong, N. (2018). Zhongguo jiayang dongwu qiyuan de zai sikao (Rethinking the origin of domesticated animals in China archaeology). *Kaogu*, **2018**(9), 113–120.

Yuan, J. & Flad, R. (2005). New zooarchaeological evidence for changes in Shang dynasty animal sacrifice. *Journal of Anthropological Archaeology*, **24**(3), 252–270.

Yuan, J., Flad, R. & Yunbing, L. (2008). Meat-acquisition patterns in the Neolithic Yangzi River Valley, China. *Antiquity*, **82**(316), 351–366.

Yuan, J. & Li, J. (2010). Hebei Xushui Nanzhuangtou yizhi chutu dongwu yicun yanjiu baogao (Research report on animal remains excavated in the Nanzhuangtou site). *Acta Archaeologica Sinica*, **2010**(3), 385–391.

Yuan, J., Pan, Y., Dong, N. & Storozum, M. (2020). Liangzhu wenhua de shengye jingji yu shenhui xingshuai (The rise and fall of the Liangzhu society in the perspective of subsistence economy). *Kaogu*, **2020**(2), 83–92.

Zeder, M. (2015). Core questions in domestication research. *Proceedings of the National Academy of Sciences*, **112**(11), 3191–3198.

Zhang, C. & Hung, H. (2013). Jiahu 1: Earliest farmers beyond the Yangtze River. *Antiquity*, **87**(335), 46–63.

Zhang, J., Chen, Z., Lan, F. et al. (2018). Henan Wuyang Jiahu yizhi zhiwu kaogu yanjiu de xin jinzhan (New progress of archaeobotanical research at the Jiahu site in Wuyang, Henan). *Kaogu*, **2018**(4), 100–110.

Zhang, J., Wang, X., Qiu, W. et al. (2011). The Paleolithic site of Longwangchan in the Middle Yellow River, China: Chronology, paleoenvironment and implications. *Journal of Archaeological Science*, **38**(7), 1537–1550.

Zhang, Q., Hou, Y., Li, X., Styring, A. & Lee-Thorp, J. (2021). Stable isotopes reveal intensive pig husbandry practices in the Middle Yellow River region by the Yangshao period (7000–5000 BP). *PLOS ONE*, **16**(10), e0257524.

Zhang, S., d'Errico, F., Backwell, L. R. et al. (2016). Ma'anshan cave and the origin of bone tool technology in China. *Journal of Archaeological Science*, **65**, 57–69.

Zhang, X., Xing, G., Chen, S., Chen, F. & Chun, C. (2010). A functional study of the points from the Hutouliang site, North China. *Acta Anthropologica Sinica*, **29**(04), 337.

Zhao, Z. (2010). New data and new issues for the study of origin of rice agriculture in China. *Archaeological and Anthropological Sciences*, **2**(2), 99–105.

Zhao, Z. (2011). New archaeobotanic data for the study of the origins of agriculture in China. *Current Anthropology*, **52**(S4), S295–S306.

Zhao, Z. & He, N. (2006). Taosi yizhi 2002 niandu faxian jieguo ji fenxi (Discoveries at the Taosi walled settlement in 2002 and their analyses). *Kaogu*, **2006**(5), 77–86.

Zhao, Z., Zhao, C., Yu, J. et al. (2020) Beijing Donghulin yizhi zhiwuyicun fuxuan jieguo (Results of floatation and analysis of floral remains from Donghulin site, Beijing). *Kaogu*, **2020**(7), 99–106.

Zheng, Y., Crawford, G. W. & Chen, X. (2014). Archaeological evidence for peach (*Prunus persica*) cultivation and domestication in China. *PLOS ONE*, **9**(9), e106595.

Zheng, Y., Crawford, G. W., Jiang, L. & Chen, X. (2016). Rice domestication revealed by reduced shattering of archaeological rice from the Lower Yangtze Valley. *Scientific Reports*, **6**(1), 28136.

Zhong, H., Zhao., C., Wei., J. & Zhao., Z. (2016). Henan Xinmi, Xinzhai yizhi 2014 nian fuxuan jieguo ji fenxi (Flotation results and analysis from the 2014 season of the Xinzhai site, Hena). *Nongye Kaogu*, **2016**(1), 21–29.

Zhou, X., Yu, J., Spengler, R. N. et al. (2020). 5,200-year-old cereal grains from the eastern Altai Mountains redate the trans-Eurasian crop exchange. *Nature Plants*, **6**(2), 78–87.

Zhu, Y. (2013). The Early Neolithic in the Central Yellow River Valley, c.7000–4000 BC. In *A companion to Chinese archaeology*. Malden, MA: Wiley, pp. 169–193.

Zuo, X., Lu, H., Jiang, L. et al. (2017). Dating rice remains through phytolith carbon-14 study reveals domestication at the beginning of the Holocene. *Proceedings of the National Academy of Sciences*, **114**(25), 6486–6491.

Acknowledgments

Special thanks is given to Gideon Shelach-Lavi, Reuven Yeshurun, Ilaria Patania and Rong Fan, who provided insights and advice on how to make this Element sharper and clearer. My great appreciation is given to the anonymous reviewers for their detailed comments on how to make this contribution clearer and sharper. The Institute for the Study of the Ancient World NYU, provided library access to many of the materials I used. Research funds and support for the editing of this Element came from the Esherick-Ye family foundation and ISF grant #1247/21.

Cambridge Elements

Archaeology of Food

Katheryn C. Twiss
Stony Brook University, New York

Katheryn C. Twiss is an archaeologist who studies ancient foodways in order to learn about social structures in the prehistoric and early historic past. Her primary areas of expertise are ancient southwest Asia, zooarchaeology, animal management and symbolism, and life in early farming communities. Dr. Twiss wrote *The Archaeology of Food: Identity, Politics, and Ideology in the Prehistoric and Historic Past* (Cambridge University Press, 2019) and edited *The Archaeology of Food And Identity (*Southern Illinois University, 2007). She has published on topics ranging from feasting in early farming villages to Mesopotamian ceremonialism.

Alexandra Livarda
Catalan Institute of Classical Archaeology

Alexandra Livarda studies human-plant interactions through time and what they reveal about agronomy, commerce, social structures, perceptions, and identities in the past. She specialises in archaeobotany, Aegean archaeology and Roman commerce, and is developing new methodological tools for the identification of past agricultural practices. Dr. Livarda has directed or co-directed archaeobotanical research in several projects, including some of the most emblematic sites in the Aegean, such as the Little Palace at Knossos and Lefkandi. She has published on a range of topics from the emergence of agriculture to the development of tastes and food commerce in the historic past.

About the Series

Elements in the Archaeology of Food showcase the vibrancy and intellectual diversity of twenty-first century archaeological research into food. Volumes reveal how food archaeology not only illuminates ancient political manoeuvres, social networks, risk management strategies, and luxurious pleasures, but also engages with modern heritage management, health, and environmental conservation strategies.

Cambridge Elements $\equiv$

Archaeology of Food

Elements in the Series

Food in Ancient China
Yitzchak Jaffe

A full series listing is available at: www.cambridge.org/EIAF